the new **Vegetarian** cookbook

THE VEGETARIAN SOCIETY'S

the new Vegetarian cookbook

Heather **Thomas**
foreword by **Linda** & **Paul McCartney**

HarperCollins*Publishers*

First published in 1997 by HarperCollins*Publishers*

Text and photographs © 1997 HarperCollins*Publishers*

A catalogue record for this book is available from the British Library.

ISBN 0 00 414016 8

For HarperCollins*Publishers*
Commissioning editor: Barbara Dixon
Designer: Clare Baggaley

Designed and produced by SP Creative Design
Editor: Heather Thomas
Art Director: Rolando Ugolini

Photography
Front cover: Simon Smith
Page 69: David Sherwin
All other photography: Huw Williams
Home Economist: Steven Wheeler

Colour reproduction by Saxon Photo Litho
Printed and bound in Italy

Contents

Foreword

By **Linda** and **Paul McCartney**

Cooking is one of the most sensual experiences – food has so many different textures, colours, aromas and flavours – and to share that with family and friends is really satisfying. And cooking vegetarian food is even more rewarding. It's the healthiest, kindest and most environmentally friendly thing that you can do for yourself, the animals and the planet. What better place to demonstrate the benefits of a vegetarian lifestyle than in the kitchen – the more that people are offered tasty vegetarian meals the more the cause will be advanced with every mouthful.

As Patrons of the Vegetarian Society, we're keen to get the message across to as many people as possible that the best food is that which doesn't hurt you or anything else. And so we're delighted to see *The New Vegetarian Cookbook*. The wonderful variety of recipes in the book demonstrates just how wide a choice of food non-meat eaters have. The book has something for everyone who loves cooking and eating delicious, innovative vegetarian food –

the recipes are fresh, healthy and colourful, and designed to appeal to the busy cook who wants to serve attractively presented meals with the minimum of fuss and effort.

Vegetarian food is naturally healthy – it looks good, tastes good and it's good for you. In fact, it's bursting with flavour and vitality. More and more people every day are embracing the vegetarian way of eating, and *The New Vegetarian Cookbook* will appeal both to newly converted and to more established, committed vegetarians. We hope you'll enjoy using this book and that it will remind everyone that being vegetarian is about living life, not ending it.

by **Heather Mairs,** Cookery School Manager, The **Vegetarian Society UK**

As a vegetarian with a huge passion for food, I am fortunate enough to have, possibly, the 'dream job' as Cookery School Manager of the Cordon Vert Cookery School. This enables me to sample one of my main pleasures in life – food, cooked with the freshest and finest ingredients – every day.

The New Vegetarian Cookbook invites you to discover the abundance of wonderful fresh produce available. It is full of delicious recipes, which are both nourishing and wholesome to the body and soul. The recipes reflect the infinite variety of vegetarian food, and explore international cuisines as well as some of the more traditional favourite dishes.

Bringing a vegetarian way of cooking into your kitchen need not be a formidable task, and the range of comprehensive dishes in this cookery book will inspire you to extend your repertoire at considerable ease, whether you are a complete beginner or a seasoned cook.

A vegetarian diet should never be thought of as a denial, as cooking without meat can be refreshingly liberating. It really is an exciting and challenging cuisine. If you possess an appreciation for good food, whether vegetarian or not, you will fully enjoy this collection of contemporary recipes. Happy cooking!

Heather Mairs.

Introduction

By eating vegetarian food, you can enjoy some delicious, sustaining dishes that respect animals and people, protect the environment and provide a healthier, safer diet. You are also eating really healthy food that tastes good, looks good and does you good.

An increasing number of people are now embracing vegetarianism and are adopting a meat-free diet as part of a healthier, and much more compassionate way of life, which does not involve the killing of animals or the abuse of the world's resources.

A well-balanced vegetarian diet provides all the nutrients your body needs for good health. Indeed, there is scientific evidence to indicate that vegetarians may be healthier than meat eaters. A vegetarian diet is typically low in saturated fat, is high in dietary fibre and complex carbohydrates, and high in protective vitamins and minerals. Medical studies have shown that vegetarians are less likely to suffer from such illnesses as heart disease, diet-related diabetes, cancer, obesity and high blood pressure.

A vegetarian diet consists of the following:
- Grains
- Pulses
- Nuts
- Seeds
- Vegetables and fruit

It may be with or without the following:
- Dairy products (cheese, milk, yogurt, butter, cream)
- Eggs

It does not include fish, poultry,

meat, game, shellfish, crustacea, or slaughter by-products such as gelatine and animal fats. Yet vegetarian food is infinitely varied, interesting, delicious, and easy to cook and prepare.

Stumbling blocks

Most new converts to the vegetarian way of life are unaware of the hidden ingredients derived from the slaughter of animals in many everyday foods. For example, gelatine (made from animal ligaments, tendons and bones) is often found in confectionery, ice cream and other dairy products. Animal fats (carcass fats) may be present in biscuits, cakes and margarine.

Many types of cheese are made with rennet, a substance which is extracted from the stomach lining of slaughtered calves. However, vegetarian alternatives, made with rennet from a microbial source, are now widely available in most supermarkets and delicatessens. For more detailed information on vegetarian ingredients, turn over to pages 10-14.

Nutrition

Just because vegetarians do not eat fish or meat, they can still get all the nutrients they need, i.e. protein, carbohydrates, fats, vitamins and minerals, by eating a healthy, balanced diet.

Protein

Protein is essential for growth and repairing our bodies. Vegetarians can get their protein from the following foods:
- **Grains and cereals:** wheat, barley, rye, oats, millet, maize and rice.
- **Nuts:** hazelnuts, Brazil nuts,

Your healthy daily vegetarian diet

On a vegetarian diet, you should eat the following every day:

Grains, cereals or potatoes	3-4 servings
Fruit and vegetables	4-5 servings
Pulses, nuts and seeds	2-3 servings
Milk, cheese, egg or soya products	2 servings
Vegetable oil and margarine or butter	small amount
Yeast extract fortified with vitamin B12	small amount

almonds, cashews, chestnuts, walnuts, peanuts, pine kernels, pecans.

■ **Seeds:** sesame, pumpkin and sunflower seeds, sprouted seeds and linseed.

■ **Pulses:** peas, beans and lentils.

■ **Dairy and soya products:** milk, cheese, yogurt and soya alternatives.

■ **Free-range eggs**

Proteins are made up of units called amino acids, and there are twenty in total. Although many of these can be made in our bodies by converting other amino acids, there are eight essential ones that can't be made and must be provided in our diet. Single plant foods don't contain all the amino acids we need in the right proportions but we can get the correct amounts by mixing different plant foods. Indeed, as long as their diet is varied and well balanced, vegetarians need not worry.

Carbohydrates

Most carbohydrates are provided by plant foods, and they are our most important source of energy. There are three types:

■ **Simple sugars:** found in fruit, milk and table sugar.

■ **Complex carbohydrates:** found in cereals and grains (bread, rice, pasta, oats, barley, millet, buckwheat and rye), and some root vegetables (potatoes and parsnips).

■ **Dietary fibre:** found in unrefined carbohydrates (wholemeal bread, brown rice, whole-grain cereals).

Fats and oils

You may be surprised to learn that we all need a little fat in our diet for good health. Fats can be saturated (hard animal fats such as butter) or

unsaturated (vegetable margarines and oils). A high intake of saturated fats has been linked to raised cholesterol levels and heart disease.

Vitamins

These organic substances are present only in tiny amounts in the food we eat. They are essential for good health and if you eat a varied diet based on fresh whole foods, you should obtain adequate amounts of the vitamins you need. The only exception is vitamin B12 which is not present in plant foods. However, most vegetarians can get as much as their bodies need from eating dairy products and free-range eggs. Here is a quick guide to vegetarian sources of vitamins:

■ **Vitamin A:** red, orange and yellow vegetables (e.g. carrots), leafy green vegetables, peaches, apricots, eggs, milk, cheese.

■ **Vitamin B:** yeasts, whole cereals, nuts, pulses, seeds, green vegetables.

■ **Vitamin C:** fresh fruit, especially citrus fruits (oranges, lemons, grapefruits), salad leaves, leafy green vegetables, blackcurrants, tomatoes, potatoes.

■ **Vitamin D:** not found in plant foods but made in the body when the skin is exposed to sunlight. Found in milk, butter, cheese, yogurt.

■ **Vitamin E:** found in vegetable oils, whole-grain cereals, eggs, soya beans, avocados.

■ **Vitamin K:** found in fresh vegetables and cereals.

Preventing loss of vitamins

1 Store vegetables in the refrigerator or a cool, dark place.
2 Prepare fruit and vegetables immediately before cooking them.
3 Don't add bicarbonate of soda to the cooking water when boiling vegetables.
4 If possible, steam vegetables above boiling water to retain their vitamin content.

Minerals

Again, these are found only in minute quantities in our food, and they have different but very important functions in our bodies.

■ **Calcium:** for healthy bones and teeth. Found in dairy produce, leafy green vegetables, nuts, seeds, beans and some dried fruit.

■ **Iron:** for healthy red blood cells. Found in leafy green vegetables, wholemeal bread, molasses, lentils, dried fruit, pulses, eggs.

■ **Zinc:** plays a role in enzyme reactions and the healthy functioning of the immune system. Found in green vegetables, whole-grain cereals, lentils, sesame and pumpkin seeds, cheese and eggs.

Vegetarian ingredients

Food groups

You should try to eat some foods from each of these four groups every day.

Group 1
Cereals and grains
Provide: energy, fibre, B vitamins, calcium, iron
Examples: bread, pasta, rice, breakfast cereals

Group 2
Pulses, nuts and seeds
Provide: protein, energy, fibre, calcium, iron, zinc
Examples: beans, chick peas, nuts, sunflower and sesame seeds

Group 3
Fruit and vegetables
Provide: calcium, iron, folate, beta-carotene, vitamin C, fibre
Examples: fruit, broccoli, carrots, peppers, onions, potatoes, tomatoes, spring greens, parsnips, dried fruit

Group 4
Soya and dairy products
Provide: protein, energy, calcium, minerals, vitamins B12 and D
Examples: tofu, textured vegetable protein (TVP), soya milk, cow's milk, cheese, yogurt

Note: You also need small amounts of plant oils, margarine or butter to provide energy, essential fatty acids and vitamins A, D and E.

Here is a brief guide to some natural, healthy ingredients that you should try to include in your diet. Eat as many natural, unprocessed foods as possible and follow the easy guidelines in the box (left). Just ensure that you eat something from each of the four major food groups featured every day.

Beans

These are a good source of protein, vitamins and minerals, and provide valuable fibre in our diet. They can be purchased dried or canned. When using dried beans, it is essential to soak them for several hours, preferably overnight, rinse them under running cold water, and then cook them in fresh water.
Beans come in all colours and sizes – little Japanese aduki beans, black beans, black-eyed beans, speckled borlotti beans, pale green broad beans, butter beans, chick peas, creamy flageolets and haricots, kidney beans, mung beans and high-protein soya beans.

Beans can be added to casseroles, soups and stews, tossed in salads, or dressed with a delicate creamy sauce or a robust tomato one. They are infinitely versatile and form the basis of many famous international dishes: Mexican frijoles (refried beans), black bean soup from the Caribbean, Jamaican rice 'n peas, and Boston baked beans.

Cereals or grains

Grains and cereals have been our staple food since ancient times, and are cultivated all over the world. They are most nutritious when the whole grains are used, as processing can reduce their vitamin and mineral content and eliminate the fibre. Thus it is better to eat wholemeal bread rather than white bread, as the natural wheat germ and bran are removed from white wheat flour.

There are many different grains and it is a good idea to try and include as many whole grains as possible in your diet. You can choose

Alcohol

Vegetarians should take care when drinking or cooking with alcohol as many alcoholic drinks are fined (clarified) with animal ingredients. These include many cask condition 'real ales' and some keg, bottled and canned beer. Wines may also have been fined with animal products, as is vintage port. Most spirits are acceptable with the possible exception of some whiskies and Spanish brandies. For more information, contact The Vegetarian Society who can recommend suitable brands.

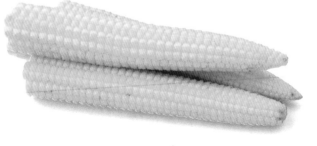

from barley (barley flour and pearl barley), buckwheat (which is often cooked like rice or made into flour), maize (the ground flour is made into Mexican tortillas and the Italian polenta), millet, oats (used in muesli, porridge and desserts), rye (as used in dark rye bread), and wheat (white and wholemeal flours, cracked wheat, and durum wheat as used in pasta).

Cheese

Cheese is a complete protein as it contains the eight essential amino acids which the body can't make itself. Rich in vitamins A, B and D, calcium and phosphorus, it is a very valuable food, although full-fat cheese is a major source of saturated fat which can lead to raised serum cholesterol levels. However, many cheeses are produced using animal rennet, an enzyme obtained from the stomachs of newly killed calves, and these are not suitable for vegetarians. But vegetarian alternatives are available, produced using microbial or fungus enzymes, and you can buy vegetarian Cheddar, Parmesan and many of your favourite cheeses. They can be bought in most supermarkets and health food stores. A list of cheeses suitable for vegetarians is available from The Vegetarian Society.

Dried fruit

This is a good source of protein, vitamins and minerals in our diet. The best dried fruits are those dried in the traditional way in the warmth of the sun. You can now buy a wide range of dried fruit, including dried apples, apricots, bananas, dates, figs, grapes (currants, raisins and sultanas), mangoes, nectarines, peaches, pears and prunes (dried plums). If the dried fruit is not guaranteed sun-dried, oil-free and unsprayed, wash in hot water before using.

Eggs

These are an important food for most vegetarians (with the exception of vegans). They are a good source of vitamins and minerals, and especially protein as their balance of essential amino acids makes ninety-five per cent of the protein available for the body to utilize. The Vegetarian Society only awards its coveted V symbol to products containing free-range eggs. You may wish to avoid battery and/or barn eggs if you have moral objections to battery farming of hens.

Eggs are extremely versatile in vegetarian cookery. They can be eaten boiled, poached, scrambled,

fried or as an essential ingredient in a whole range of savoury and sweet dishes, from soufflés and quiches to omelettes and cakes.

Fruit

Although we can now enjoy a wide range of fresh fruit all the year round, one of the delights of a healthy vegetarian diet is eating the new fruits as they come into season – the first strawberries of summer, blackberries in the autumn, tangerines at Christmas, and gooseberries and rhubarb in the late spring. Fresh fruit is healthy, low in calories, a good source of vitamins and a delicious way to end a meal. You will find some wonderful recipes in this book for fruit desserts. Choose firm, undamaged fruit with shining skin and always wash it thoroughly before using as it may have been sprayed with insecticides. Better still, buy organically grown fruit if possible.

Gelatine

This gelling agent is made from animal ligaments, bones, skin and tendons which have been boiled in water. Gelatine is present in many foods, including some margarines, ice creams and low-fat yogurts so you should always read labels carefully before buying these food products. You can use vegetarian alternatives such as agar agar and Gelozone instead.

Herbs

Fresh or dried, herbs can be used to flavour and enhance many vegetarian dishes. If you have a garden, however small, it is a good idea to grow some herbs yourself. As well as the usual thyme, parsley, sage, rosemary, mint and chives, you could experiment with dill, tarragon, coriander, basil, fennel, oregano and lemon balm. This will not only save you money buying small packets of herbs in the supermarket but will also bring endless pleasure – a new dimension to your cooking and wonderful scents and aromas to your garden.

Honey

Honey is made by bees collecting the nectar from flowers, and the composition, flavour and appearance of a particular type of honey will vary according to the flowers, the season, the weather and the location. Honey contains vitamins B and C together with important minerals, and has long been used in medicine and healing. It can be used to replace sugar in many sweet dishes. However, it is avoided by most vegans.

Lentils

One of the oldest pulses, lentils are the small seeds of an Eastern Mediterranean plant. The most commonly used lentils are the orange-red Egyptian or Syrian ones, but you can also buy the brownish Continental lentils and little greenish-black Puy lentils, which are now becoming more fashionable. Unlike beans, they do not require soaking before cooking. For the vegetarian, they are a good source of protein (although they are not a complete protein). They can be used in soups and stews, curries and salads.

Margarine

Vegetarians should note that many margarines contain animal fats, fish oils, E numbers, whey and gelatine (made from animal ligaments, tendons and bones). A list of suitable brands of margarine can be obtained from The Vegetarian Society.

Milk

Milk is full of goodness and an important natural ingredient in a well-balanced diet. Most vegetarians, with the exception of vegans, eat dairy products (milk, cheese and yogurt). Vegans can substitute soya milk. Cow's milk is a good source of protein, carbohydrates and calcium, other minerals and vitamins. Although young children should have whole milk, many adults may prefer to use semi-skimmed or skimmed milk with their lower fat content. They can be substituted for whole milk in most recipes but the results will not be so creamy.

Nuts

Nuts are exceptionally high in protein and form an important part of the vegetarian diet, although they do have a high fat content. Always try to buy organic nuts which have not been treated with preservatives. Almonds, Brazil nuts, cashews, coconut, hazelnuts, peanuts, pecans, pine nuts, pistachios, chestnuts and walnuts can all add interest and variety to our daily diet. The classic vegetarian dish utilizing nuts is nut roast, but you can also mix them into rice and pasta dishes, salads and curries. They can be chopped or ground and mixed with flour and butter to make a crumble topping for savoury dishes and puddings. When cooking with nuts, you should be aware that some people are allergic to them and you should check with your guests first.

Pasta

This is a marvellously versatile, healthy fast food which can be used in many vegetarian dishes – layered with vegetables and baked (as in lasagne and cannelloni), or tossed with fresh vegetable sauces. You can now buy a wide range of pasta, either fresh or dried, or you can make it yourself. Always cook pasta in plenty of lightly salted boiling water until it is just tender (*al dente*). It should never be soft or mushy, nor too firm and chewy.

Rice

Eaten throughout the world, rice contains starch, protein, B vitamins and minerals. The best rice to eat is whole-grain brown rice, which has a pleasantly nutty texture and flavour. However, white rice is the basis for most classic rice dishes, including risotto, paella and pilaffs. Use the plump Italian Arborio rice in risotto, and the fluffy Basmati rice for curries. Scented Thai jasmine rice is the perfect accompaniment to vegetable stir-fries. You can also

buy wild rice, which is not really a cereal at all but the green seeds of a wild grass. it is grown in the United States and harvested by the native American Indians.

Seeds

Pumpkin, sesame and sunflower seeds are all surprisingly rich in vitamins and minerals, and you should try to include them in your diet every day. You can eat them as a snack, scatter them over salads, or sprinkle them over bread loaves and rolls before baking. In the eastern Mediterranean, sesame seeds are ground into a paste and used in creamy tahini and hummus.

Spices

These add excitement and interest to many vegetarian dishes, both sweet and savoury. If possible, use them freshly ground rather than buying

them ready-ground. It really does make a difference to the flavour of a dish. You can grind them yourself in a pestle and mortar or an electric grinder. Many of the recipes in this book call for spices, especially allspice (berries), cinnamon (sticks), cloves, coriander, cumin, ginger (fresh root or dried), mace, nutmeg, pepper and vanilla (extract or the pod).

Vegetables

The most versatile and interesting of all foods, vegetables provide a rich source of nutrients in our diet – starch, protein, minerals and vitamins. They come in such an enormous array of colours, textures and flavours, from the more familiar root vegetables (potatoes, carrots, turnips, swedes, parsnips) and leafy green vegetables (cabbage, Brussels sprouts, spring greens, spinach) to salad vegetables and the more exotic peppers, aubergines and pumpkins. You can have fun experimenting with so many unusual vegetables, such as celeriac, Swiss chard, Jerusalem artichokes and okra.

Always remember when buying vegetables that they should look and smell fresh, and have a bright, wholesome appearance. They should be firm and crisp, never dry or soft with curling, wilted leaves. Many stores now offer a good range of organically grown vegetables and you should try to buy these, subject to availability and budget. Always wash vegetables thoroughly before using to wash away dirt and traces of sprays. The secret of serving delicious vegetables with maximum nutritional content is never to overcook them.

Steaming above boiling water is a good way of cooking delicate vegetables such as broccoli and cauliflower florets, and also ensures minimal vitamin loss. If boiling vegetables, cook them in the minimum of water until they are just tender but still retain some natural crispness and bite. Keep the pan uncovered to help retain their bright green colour. Stir-frying is another excellent cooking method for peppers, mange-tout, spring onions and green beans as the vegetables are tossed and stirred quickly in a little oil over high heat for only a few minutes.

Yogurt

Vegetarians should buy organic wholemilk yogurt, which is made with milk from dairy farms that meet the requirements of the Soil Association. Yogurt is an important healthy food due to its ability to encourage beneficial organisms to grow in the digestive system. The friendly lactobacillus in the yogurt can help maintain the balance of the intestinal microflora and, indeed, manufactures many of the B vitamins needed in the intestine to create a healthy environment.

Cooking methods

Every vegetarian knows that the healthiest cooking methods, which retain maximum nutrients in our food, are steaming, grilling and stir-frying. Vegetables respond well to these methods, and you will find delicious recipes for grilled, barbecued and stir-fried dishes in this book.

Grilling

Grilled food cooks rapidly when exposed to intense heat. The crisp, outer crust seals in moisture and helps retain nutrients, especially minerals and fat-soluble vitamins which can be diminished by boiling, frying or roasting. Grilling is a healthy, low-fat cooking method, as the food to be grilled is brushed only very lightly with the minimum of oil or marinade. Vegetables can be cooked under a conventional gas or electric grill or, better still, over charcoal. Grilling over hot coals imparts a delicious smoky flavour to the food.

Stir-frying

A quick and easy way of cooking vegetables in the minimum of oil in a wok or a large deep frying pan. Stir-frying must always be performed over fierce heat to seal in the flavour of the vegetables as they come into contact with the hot wok. Foods to be stir-fried are always cut into thin strips or small pieces so that more of their surfaces are exposed to the oil and contact the wok, making them cook quickly. Timing is important as sometimes the food cooks in seconds rather than minutes, and although stir-fried vegetables should be just tender, they should retain their natural crispness and 'bite'. The best oils to use are sesame oil, groundnut oil or sunflower oil.

Steaming

This is a gentle, healthy way of cooking in which the food does not come into direct contact with the simmering water below but cooks in the steam. Many vegetables, especially the watery ones like courgettes, marrow and pumpkin, taste better steamed than boiled. Broccoli florets and mange-tout are delicious steamed and retain their lovely fresh green colour. Timing is essential and it is important not to overcook steamed vegetables, so keep an eye on them and don't forget them. If you don't have a steamer, you can improvise with a large colander placed over a saucepan of simmering water and covered with a lid.

Roasting

Roasted seasonal vegetables are now extremely fashionable, but the tradition of roasting vegetables is very old. Root vegetables have long been cooked in Britain around the Sunday roast, and the custom of roasting peppers, aubergines, onions and tomatoes in olive oil has always been prevalent in the Spanish countryside. When roasting, always make sure that the oven is preheated to the correct temperature. Sprinkle the vegetables of your choice with good-quality olive oil and scatter them with fresh herbs. If wished, you can tuck some garlic cloves down between the vegetables and then grind some sea salt and black pepper over the top. Delicious!

Frying

Although vegetable tempura, fritters and croquettes taste wonderful, deep-frying in hot oil is not a very healthy way of cooking food which tends to absorb a lot of fat. Food to be deep-fried needs to be coated in flour, breadcrumbs or batter first to give it a protective covering. Always fry at 190°C/375°F until crisp and golden, then remove with a slotted spoon and drain on absorbent kitchen paper to soak up excess oil before serving. Shallow-frying uses less oil but, again, make sure that the oil is really hot before adding the food and drain it thoroughly on kitchen paper before serving.

Equipment

To be successful in vegetarian cookery, you need the right tools for the job. It is not necessary to invest in an expensive array of electronic gadgetry (juice extractors, ice-cream makers, pasta machines and the like) but you should have the following:

- Sharp knives for cutting up vegetables etc.
- Good-quality heavy-based saucepans
- A wok for stir-frying
- A blender or food processor for puréeing soups, vegetables etc.
- A steamer (optional) for steaming vegetables
- A cast-iron enamelled casserole which can be used on the hob or in the oven
- Baking sheets, quiche tins and ovenproof dishes for baking and gratins
- A balloon whisk and electric hand whisk

Soups & Starters

Easy to make, filling and nutritious, many of these soups can be served with bread and cheese as a light meal. Alternatively, you can try one of the delicious vegetable first courses, including deep-fried snacks and fritters, stuffed vegetables and blinis.

Cajun **Black Bean** Soup

The brilliant salsa garnish lifts this soup from the ordinary into the sublime. You can serve the salsa with Mexican food or as a dip for tortilla chips and raw vegetables.

225 g/8 oz black beans
2 tablespoons olive oil
1 onion, chopped
1 carrot, diced
1 leek, cleaned, trimmed and chopped
2 garlic cloves, crushed
1 red chilli, seeded and chopped
1 teaspoon cumin seeds
1 teaspoon coriander seeds
600 ml/2 pints vegetable stock
3 tablespoons tomato purée
salt and freshly ground black pepper
sour cream, to garnish

FOR THE SALSA:
2 garlic cloves
3 tomatoes, skinned, seeded and chopped
1 red onion, finely chopped
1 small red pepper, roasted, skinned, seeded and chopped
1 red chilli, seeded and finely chopped
2 tablespoons chopped fresh coriander
juice of 1/2 lime
1 tablespoon olive oil
1/2 avocado, peeled and diced
freshly ground black pepper

1 Soak the black beans in water overnight. Drain and rinse well under running cold water. Set aside.

2 Heat the olive oil in a large saucepan and sauté the onion, carrot, leek and garlic over gentle heat until softened. Add the chilli.

3 Put the cumin and coriander seeds on a baking sheet and roast in a preheated oven at 180°C, 350°F, Gas Mark 4 for 5 minutes. Remove and grind to a powder. Add to the vegetables in the pan.

4 Add the vegetable stock, the black beans and tomato purée, stirring well. Bring to the boil, then reduce the heat and simmer very gently for 2 hours. Take out some of the cooked black beans and set aside to use in the salsa.

5 Purée the soup in a blender or food processor. Season to taste and reheat. Serve hot with the salsa and sour cream.

6 To make the salsa: roast the garlic cloves in their skins, then peel and mash with a fork. Mix with the remaining ingredients.

Serves 6

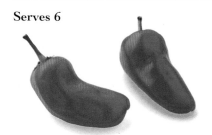

Opposite: Cajun Black Bean Soup

Celeriac and Stilton Soup

600 g/1¼ lb celeriac, peeled
and cubed
1 onion, finely chopped
25 g/1 oz butter
1 litre/1¾ pints vegetable stock
few sprigs of thyme
115 g/4 oz Stilton, or
other blue cheese
150 ml/¼ pint single cream
salt and freshly ground black pepper
herb croûtons, to garnish
(see page 138)

Celeriac is one of the most subtly flavoured root vegetables and is still unfamiliar to many people, but it makes a warming and delicious winter soup.

1 Sauté the celeriac and onion in the butter over gentle heat, until they have softened. Make sure that the celeriac and onion do not colour.

2 Add the vegetable stock and ___ ___ ___ ___ e boil.

Reduce the heat to a gentle simmer, cover the saucepan and cook very gently for 20 minutes.

3 Purée the soup in a blender or food processor, then return to the pan. Crumble the Stilton into the soup and heat very gently, stirring until the Stilton melts into the soup. Stir in the cream and season to taste. Serve garnished with herb croûtons.

Serves 4-6

very good.
didn't use
cream

___ ___om Soup

___ ___ now stocked by most supermarkets. However, ___ ___y, you could substitute oyster or shiitake ___ ___d porcini which have been soaked in boiling ___ ___ng liquid instead of stock.

1
2 ga___
200 g/___
mus___
115 g___
(cha___
gir___
900 ml/___
pinch of nutmeg
150 ml/¼ pint milk
75 ml/3 fl oz Marsala
salt and freshly ground
black pepper
115 ml/4 fl oz double cream or
crème fraîche

___ ___large saucepan ___ ___d garlic until ___ ___tir in the ___ ___gently for 5 minutes.

2 Add the hot vegetable stock and a pinch of nutmeg. Bring to a simmer, stir in the milk and Marsala, and then simmer gently for 45 minutes, stirring occasionally.

3 Remove a few of the mushrooms with a slotted spoon and set aside for the garnish. Purée the soup in a blender or food processor and return to the pan. Season to taste, stir in the cream or crème fraîche and reheat gently. Serve in soup bowls, garnished with the reserved mushrooms.

Serves 6

Tuscan **Bean** Soup

225 g/8 oz dried cannellini beans
75 ml/3 fl oz olive oil
1 onion, chopped
1 leek, cleaned, trimmed
and chopped
2 carrots, chopped
2 sticks celery, chopped
2 potatoes, cubed
1 bulb fennel, chopped
225 g/8 oz tomatoes, skinned
and chopped
2 garlic cloves, crushed
1.2 litres/2 pints vegetable stock
450 g/1 lb greens or dark green
cabbage, shredded
salt and freshly ground
black pepper

TO GARNISH:
6 slices crusty white bread
1-2 garlic cloves, peeled
olive oil

A thick, robust peasant soup, in Tuscany this is known as *la Ribollita*, and it is made overnight. To be authentic, it must be made with white cannellini beans and cabbage. In Italy, they use *cavolo nero*, but you can cheat with a dark green cabbage, some greens or even Swiss chard.

1 Soak the beans in cold water overnight, or for at least 5 hours. Drain and rinse the beans under running cold water.

2 Heat the olive oil in a large saucepan and add the onion, leek, carrots, celery, potatoes, fennel and tomatoes. Stew the vegetables gently in the olive oil for 8-10 minutes. Stir in the garlic and cook for 2 minutes.

3 Add the vegetable stock and the drained beans, bring to the boil, then reduce the heat to a simmer. Cook very gently for 1 hour and then stir in the greens or cabbage. Continue cooking for 15-20 minutes until the beans are cooked and tender.

4 Season the soup to taste with salt and pepper, remove from the heat and cover the pan with a lid. Set aside in a cool place until the next day.

5 The following day, reheat the soup, and while it is heating through prepare the garnish. Rub the slices of bread with the garlic cloves and brush lightly with a little olive oil. Pop under a hot grill to toast them.

6 Ladle the soup into bowls and top each one with a slice of garlic bread. Hand a small jug of olive oil round separately for people to trickle over the top if wished.

Serves 4

Pumpkin Soup

2 onions, finely chopped
2 garlic cloves, crushed
3 tablespoons olive oil
1.5 kg/3 lb wedge of pumpkin
900 ml/1 1/2 pints vegetable stock
1 teaspoon chopped fresh sage
pinch of sugar
salt and freshly ground
black pepper
50 g/2 oz grated Chedder cheese
garlic croûtons, to garnish
(see page 138)

This is a traditional French country soup, but you can easily transform it into a West Indian favourite by omitting the cheese and stirring in a dash of hot pepper sauce just before serving.

1 Sauté the onions and garlic in the olive oil in a large saucepan over low heat until soft and translucent.

2 Remove the seeds from the pumpkin and cut off the rind. Cut the flesh of the pumpkin into small cubes and add to the onions in the pan. Cook gently for 5 minutes.

3 Add the vegetable stock, sage and sugar, and simmer over low heat for 30-40 minutes, until the pumpkin is tender and starts to break up.

4 Purée the soup in a blender or food processor until smooth. Return to the pan and reheat. Season to taste with salt and pepper, and serve the soup sprinkled with grated cheese and garlic croûtons.

Serves 6

Spicy **Carrot** and Cumin Soup

A great soup for warming you up on a cold autumnal evening. You can vary the flavour by substituting parsnip for some of the carrot.

25 g /1 oz butter
600 g/1¼ lb carrots, diced
1 onion, finely chopped
2 garlic cloves, crushed
1 potato, diced
½ teaspoon ground cumin
½ teaspoon ground nutmeg
pinch each of ground ginger, turmeric and paprika
¼ teaspoon ground coriander
1 teaspoon soft brown sugar
900 ml/1½ pints vegetable stock
salt and pepper
150 ml/¼ pint milk
Greek yogurt and chopped parsley or coriander, to garnish

1 Melt the butter in a large saucepan and stir in the carrots, onion, garlic and potato. Cook gently over low heat until softened.

2 Stir in all the spices and cook over low heat for 2-3 minutes. Add the brown sugar and vegetable stock and bring to the boil. Reduce the heat immediately and simmer for 15-20 minutes, until tender.

3 Purée the soup in a blender or food processor until it has a smooth texture. Return to the pan, season to taste and stir in the milk. Reheat the soup over low heat.

4 Serve the soup topped with a swirl of yogurt and garnish with a sprinkling of parsley or coriander.

Serves 6

Soupe au **Pistou**

This is the ultimate in bean and vegetable soups – a simple Provençal clear soup made special by the addition of garlicky pistou sauce stirred in at the table. For the best results, make the pistou yourself and don't be tempted to buy a ready-made pesto from the supermarket.

225 g/8 oz dried haricot beans
2 tablespoons olive oil
2 carrots, diced
2 leeks, cleaned, trimmed and diced
2 sticks celery, diced
350 g/12 oz tomatoes, skinned and chopped
1.2 litres/2 pints water
2 large potatoes, peeled and diced
225 g/8 oz thin green beans, trimmed and cut into 1-cm/½-in lengths
225 g/8 oz courgettes, diced
50 g/2 oz vermicelli
salt and freshly ground black pepper

FOR THE PISTOU:
4 garlic cloves, peeled
pinch of salt
20-25 basil leaves
115 g/4 oz vegetarian Parmesan cheese
115 ml/4 fl oz olive oil

1 Put the beans in a bowl, cover with cold water and soak overnight. Drain the beans and tip them into a large saucepan. Cover with plenty of fresh water and bring to the boil. Boil for 10 minutes, skimming off any scum that rises to the surface. Simmer for 1 hour until the beans are tender, then drain.

2 Heat the olive oil in a large saucepan and stir in the carrots, leeks, celery and tomatoes. Cook gently for 2-3 minutes. Add the water and bring to the boil. Reduce the heat and simmer for 15 minutes.

3 Add the potatoes, green beans, courgettes and vermicelli, and simmer gently for about 15 minutes.

The vegetables should be tender but still retain their shape. Season to taste with salt and pepper.

4 While the soup is cooking, make the pistou. Put the garlic, salt and basil in a blender or food processor and process to a purée. Add the Parmesan cheese, process again and then add the olive oil through the feed tube in a thin steady trickle until the mixture is well blended. You should end up with a thick bright green paste. Transfer to a bowl.

5 Stir the pistou into the soup just before serving, or hand it separately and let your guests help themselves. Serve with crusty bread.

Serves 6

Spicy **Callaloo**

In the West Indies, this soup is made with fresh callaloo leaves, which are sometimes available in Britain from West Indian shops. Spinach makes a good substitute.

450 g/1 lb fresh callaloo or spinach leaves
1 large onion, finely chopped
2 garlic cloves, crushed
3 tablespoons groundnut or olive oil
1 red chilli, seeded and finely chopped
1 teaspoon turmeric
225 g/8 oz fresh okra, trimmed and thinly sliced
900 ml/1½ pints vegetable stock
few strands of saffron
400 ml/14 fl oz coconut milk
salt and freshly ground black pepper
juice of ½ lime
dash of hot pepper sauce

1 Wash the callaloo or spinach leaves thoroughly to remove any dirt. Drain well, shake dry and discard any tough stems. Chop the leaves and set aside.

2 Sauté the onion and garlic in the groundnut or olive oil in a large saucepan. Cook for 5 minutes until soft and translucent. Stir in the chilli and turmeric and cook for 1-2 minutes.

3 Add the okra and callaloo or spinach leaves and stir over medium heat until the leaves start to wilt and turn bright green. Add the vegetable stock and saffron and bring to a simmer. Cover the pan and simmer for 20 minutes.

4 Stir in the coconut milk and continue cooking for 5-10 minutes. Season to taste and, just before serving, stir in the lime juice and a dash of hot pepper sauce.

Serves 6

Moroccan **Harira**

This colourful soup is traditionally made during Ramadan and is consumed at sunset when the daily fast comes to an end. It is refreshing and comforting.

175 g/6 oz dried chick peas
3 tablespoons olive oil
1 onion, chopped
1 stick celery, chopped
1 teaspoon ground cinnamon
1 teaspoon turmeric
1 teaspoon paprika
450 g/1 lb tomatoes, skinned and chopped
115 g/4 oz lentils
1.2 litres/2 pints vegetable stock
50 g/2 oz vermicelli
salt and freshly ground black pepper
few sprigs of fresh coriander, chopped
few sprigs of flat-leaf parsley, chopped
lemon wedges and harissa (optional), to serve

1 Put the chick peas in a bowl, cover with cold water and soak overnight. The following day, drain them and rinse under running cold water. Set aside.

2 Heat the oil in a large saucepan and cook the onion and celery over low heat until softened. Stir in the spices and cook for 2-3 minutes. Add the tomatoes and lentils and stir well.

3 Add the chick peas and cook gently for about 5 minutes. Add the vegetable stock and then simmer gently for 1½-2 hours, until the chick peas are tender and cooked.

4 Add the vermicelli and simmer for a further 15 minutes. Season to taste with salt and pepper, and stir in the chopped coriander and parsley. Serve hot with lemon wedges and a little bowl of harissa (optional).

Serves 6

Dolmades

Serves 6

Lemon-scented vine leaves rolled around a spicy rice stuffing are a traditional Middle Eastern *meze*. If you have a vine in your garden, you can enjoy the luxury of using fresh leaves. However, most of us will have to fall back on pickled or canned ones which are now widely available from most supermarket's and or delicatessen.

175 g/6 oz fresh or pickled vine leaves
115 g/4 oz long-grain rice
1 small onion, finely chopped
1 tomato, skinned, seeded and chopped
few sprigs of parsley, finely chopped
1 tablespoon chopped mint
1 tablespoon snipped chives
1/4 teaspoon each of ground cinnamon, allspice and cumin
25 g/1 oz pine nuts
75 g/3 oz currants
salt and freshly ground black pepper
2 garlic cloves, sliced
50 ml/2 fl oz olive oil
150 ml/1/4 pint water
1 teaspoon sugar
juice of 1 lemon
olive oil and lemon juice, to serve

Line the base of a heavy saucepan with any broken or left-over leaves and pack in the dolmades tightly in layers. Tuck the sliced garlic in between the dolmades.

4 Pour in the olive oil, water, sugar and lemon juice, press a plate down over the top and cover the pan with a lid. Simmer gently for 1½ hours, checking from time to time and adding more boiling water if necessary, as it is absorbed by the filling. Leave in the pan to cool before removing the dolmades. Serve cold dressed with a little olive oil and lemon juice.

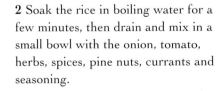

1 If you are using fresh vine leaves, boil them for 3-4 minutes in water and then drain. Pickled vine leaves should be soaked in hot water for 20-30 minutes, then removed and patted dry with kitchen paper. Remove the stalks from the leaves and spread them out with the veined underside facing upwards.

2 Soak the rice in boiling water for a few minutes, then drain and mix in a small bowl with the onion, tomato, herbs, spices, pine nuts, currants and seasoning.

3 Place a little of the filling in the centre of each leaf, fold the sides over into the middle and roll up.

Mushrooms on Polenta Croûtes

This is a novel and spectacular way to serve creamed mushrooms – on crisp golden polenta rectangles. Serve it as a first course, or as a light meal with a crisp green salad.

25 g/1 oz butter
2 shallots, finely chopped
450 g/1 lb button mushrooms, quartered
115 ml/4 fl oz Madeira or Marsala
200 ml/7 fl oz whipping cream
squeeze of lemon juice
salt and freshly ground black pepper
1 tablespoon chopped parsley

FOR THE CROÛTES:
1 litre/1³/4 pints water
salt
175 g/6 oz polenta
25 g/1 oz unsalted butter
olive oil for frying

1 Make the polenta croûtes: bring the water and salt to the boil in a large saucepan. Gradually add the polenta in a steady, thin stream, whisking all the time. Reduce the heat to a bare simmer – as low as it will go – and continue stirring and beating the polenta with a wooden spoon for about 15 minutes, until the polenta is thick and smooth and has absorbed all the liquid. It should leave the sides of the pan clean.

2 Stir in the butter thoroughly and pour the polenta into an oiled rectangular tin. Smooth the surface and set aside to cool.

3 When cold, cut the polenta into 12 rectangles. Heat the olive oil and fry the polenta croûtes on both sides until crisp and golden. Drain on kitchen paper and keep warm while you prepare the mushroom topping.

4 Melt the butter and gently cook the shallots until soft and golden. Add the mushrooms and cook until lightly golden. Add the Madeira or Marsala and cook rapidly until the liquid evaporates and turns syrupy. Stir in the cream and simmer until the sauce thickens. Season with lemon juice and salt and pepper.

5 Top the polenta croûtes with the creamed mushrooms and serve sprinkled with chopped parsley.

Serves 4

Sicilian **Caponata**

3 aubergines, cut into 1.25-cm/¹/2-in dice
1 onion, thinly sliced
4 tablespoons olive oil
2 sticks celery, diced
150 ml/¹/4 pint passata (sieved tomatoes)
3 tablespoons wine vinegar
1 tablespoon sugar
1 red pepper, seeded and thinly sliced

1 yellow pepper, seeded and thinly sliced
50 g/2 oz capers, roughly chopped
50 g/2 oz black olives, pitted
50 g/2 oz green olives, pitted
2 tablespoons pine nuts
salt and freshly ground black pepper
2 tablespoons chopped parsley

This is the Sicilian 'sweet and sour' way of cooking aubergines with peppers, capers and olives. It makes a wonderful first course for summer entertaining. The flavours improve if the caponata is made the day before it is eaten.

1 Put the aubergines in a colander, sprinkle with salt and set aside for 20 minutes to drain and exude their bitter juices. Rinse well under running cold water and pat dry with kitchen paper.

2 Sauté the onion in the olive oil until soft and translucent. Add the celery and cook for 3 minutes to soften. Stir in the aubergine and cook, stirring occasionally, for a few more minutes.

3 Add the passata, wine vinegar, sugar, red and yellow peppers, capers, olives and pine nuts, and cook gently over low heat until the vegetables are tender. Season to taste with salt and pepper.

4 Transfer the mixture to a serving dish and set aside to cool. The

Mushrooms on Polenta Croûtes

caponata is best when eaten at room temperature rather than cold from the refrigerator. Serve it sprinkled with chopped parsley.

Serves 4

Blinis with Sun-dried Tomatoes

115 g/4 oz buckwheat flour
115 g/4 oz strong white
bread flour
1 teaspoon salt
350 ml/12 fl oz warm milk
15 g/½ oz fresh yeast
1 teaspoon sugar
2 eggs, separated
2 tablespoons soured cream
unsalted butter for frying

FOR THE TOPPING:
25 g/1 oz melted butter
½ red onion, finely chopped
25 g/1 oz sun-dried tomatoes,
cut into slivers
freshly ground black pepper
soured cream and snipped
chives, to garnish

What could be more opulent than traditional Russian blinis topped with melted butter, diced onion, sun-dried tomatoes and generous dollops of soured cream? For an alternative, try thinly sliced avocado and creamy goat's cheese.

1 Sift the flours and salt into a mixing bowl. Warm the milk to blood heat, and crumble in the yeast. Add the sugar and egg yolks and stir well. Make a well in the centre of the flours and pour in the yeast mixture and soured cream. Mix well.

2 Cover the bowl and leave in a warm place for about 1 hour, until the batter gets thicker and some bubbles appear on the surface.

3 Whisk the egg whites until stiff and gently fold into the batter.

4 Heat a tiny knob of butter in a non-stick pan and pour in 2 tablespoons of the batter. Fry until the underside is set and golden-brown. Flip over and cook the other side. Cook the remaining blinis in the same way and keep warm until required.

5 Serve the blinis warm with melted butter, red onion, sun-dried tomatoes and a good grinding of black pepper. Top with a spoonful of soured cream and some snipped chives.

Serves 6

Trio of Stuffed Vegetables

Stuffed colourful vegetables are a feature of Mediterranean cooking and make a delicious first course. Serve them hot or cold with a garnish of crisp bitter salad leaves.

1 Cut the aubergines, peppers and courgettes in half lengthways. Scoop out the flesh from the aubergines and courgettes and chop roughly. Remove the seeds and stalks from the peppers.

2 Heat 3 tablespoons of the olive oil and sauté the onion and garlic until soft and translucent. Add the aubergine and courgette flesh and cook gently until soft and golden.

3 Remove from the heat and stir in the tomatoes, breadcrumbs, pine

2 aubergines
1 large yellow pepper
1 large red pepper
2 courgettes
7 tablespoons extra-virgin olive oil
1 onion, finely chopped
2 garlic cloves, crushed
350 g/12 oz tomatoes, skinned
and chopped
50 g/2 oz fresh white breadcrumbs
2 tablespoons pine nuts
2 tablespoons chopped capers
50 g/2 oz vegetarian Parmesan cheese
2 tablespoons chopped parsley
or marjoram
salt and freshly ground black pepper
rocket, watercress and radicchio,
to garnish

nuts, capers, Parmesan cheese, herbs and seasoning to taste.

4 Fill the aubergine, pepper and courgette shells with the stuffing mixture, smoothing the tops. Arrange in a well-oiled ovenproof dish and drizzle the remaining olive oil over the top.

5 Bake the stuffed vegetables in a preheated oven at 200°C, 400°F, Gas Mark 6 for about 45 minutes, until golden brown. Take care that they do not burn. Serve warm or cold with a garnish of salad leaves and watercress.

Serves 6

Char-grilled **Pepper** Salad

4 red, green and yellow peppers

FOR THE OLIVE OIL
DRESSING:
4 tablespoons fruity green
olive oil
2 garlic cloves, crushed
freshly ground sea salt and
black pepper
2 tablespoons chopped parsley

FOR THE SALSA VERDE:
115 g/4 oz capers, chopped
2 garlic cloves, crushed
2 teaspoons whole-grain
Dijon mustard
6 tablespoons olive oil
2 tablespoons white wine vinegar
2 tablespoons chopped marjoram
3 tablespoons chopped parsley
salt and freshly ground
black pepper

Grilling brings out the natural sweetness and juiciness of peppers. You can cook the peppers under a grill or, better still, barbecue them over hot coals until the skin is charred. Serve with a simple dressing of olive oil and garlic or a piquant salsa verde.

1 Place the peppers under a hot grill and cook them, turning occasionally, until they are charred and blistered. Remove and place in a polythene bag. Leave to cool, then peel away the skins.

2 Cut the peppers open and remove the seeds. Cut the flesh into strips and arrange in a serving dish. Sprinkle with olive oil and garlic. Season with salt and pepper and scatter the parsley over the top.

3 Alternatively, serve the peppers warm with the salsa verde. To make the salsa verde, mix all the ingredients together until well

blended. Spoon a little over the peppers and serve the rest separately. Eat with crusty bread.

Serves 4-6

Deep-fried **Camembert**

These little golden fritters, oozing with melted cheese, can be served in the French style with a salad of dressed bitter leaves, some olives and baby gherkins, or with a fresh, tart cranberry sauce.

2 boxes just ripe Camembert
cheese
1 large egg, beaten
1 tablespoon flour
115 g/4 oz fresh breadcrumbs
vegetable oil, for deep-frying

FOR THE CRANBERRY SAUCE:
200 ml/7 fl oz water
75 g/3 oz caster sugar
225 g/8 oz fresh cranberries
juice of 1 orange

1 Make the cranberry sauce. Put the water and sugar in a saucepan and stir over low heat until the sugar dissolves. Bring to the boil and tip in the cranberries. Bring back to the boil, then simmer for 5 minutes, until the berries start popping. Cover the pan and set aside to cool. When cold and thick, stir the orange juice into the sauce. Refrigerate until required.

2 Cut each Camembert cheese into 6 triangles. Dip them in the beaten egg, shaking off any excess, and then into the flour and breadcrumbs.

3 Heat the vegetable oil in a large, heavy saucepan or deep-fat fryer to 190°C, 375°F, and quickly fry the breadcrumbed Camembert triangles, a few at a time, until crisp and golden brown. Remove with a slotted spoon, drain on kitchen paper and keep warm while you fry the remaining triangles in the same way.

4 Serve the Camembert immediately with the cranberry sauce and a garnish of bitter salad leaves.

Serves 4

Falafel Snacks

2 x 400-g/14-oz cans chick peas
1 onion, finely chopped
4 garlic cloves, crushed
1 teaspoon ground cumin
1 teaspoon ground coriander
1 small red chilli, seeded and finely chopped (optional)
2 tablespoons plain flour
1/4 teaspoon baking powder
1 tablespoon chopped fresh coriander

2 tablespoons chopped parsley
salt and freshly ground black pepper
oil for deep-frying

TO SERVE:
150 ml/5 fl oz natural yogurt
3 tablespoons chopped mint
tahini
lemon wedges

These crisp, spicy snacks are popular street food in Israel and throughout the Middle East. To be authentic, you should use dried chick peas and soak them overnight, but this is both tedious and time-consuming for busy cooks. This quick and simple recipe uses canned chick peas to make your life easier.

1 Drain the chick peas and rinse in a colander under running cold water. Dry on kitchen paper and tip into a food processor with the onion, garlic, cumin, ground coriander and chilli, if using. Process until thick and smooth. Add the flour, baking powder, herbs and seasoning, and process quickly until well-blended.

2 Transfer the mixture to a bowl, and then roll between your floured hands into little balls. Deep-fry the falafel in hot oil until golden brown and crisp. Remove with a slotted spoon and drain on kitchen paper.

3 Serve hot with a bowl of yogurt blended with chopped mint, or some tahini and lemon wedges.

Serves 4

Feta Cheese Pastries

These little Greek pastries oozing with feta cheese melt in the mouth and can be served as a first course or as canapés with drinks. They can be made in advance and then reheated in a low oven.

400 g/14 oz packet filo pastry
75 g/3 oz melted butter

FOR THE FILLING:
2 eggs, lightly beaten
175 g/6 oz feta cheese, crumbled
115 g/4 oz grated Swiss or vegetarian Parmesan cheese
2 tablespoons chopped flat-leaf parsley
freshly ground black pepper
freshly grated nutmeg

1 Make the feta cheese filling. Mix the beaten eggs with the cheeses, parsley, black pepper and nutmeg. Do not add any salt as the feta is salty enough.

2 Take one of the filo pastry sheets and brush lightly with melted butter. Cut the sheet into 3 long strips. Fold each strip over lengthways and brush with more butter. Place a small spoonful of the filling at one end of the strip and fold the pastry over to make a triangle. Fold over again in this way, and continue folding until the strip is used up and you have a thick triangle. Brush with more melted butter and place on a greased baking sheet. Make the remaining pastries in the same way.

3 Cook in a preheated oven at 190°C, 375°F, Gas Mark 5 for 15-20 minutes, until the pastries are crisp and golden. Serve hot.

Serves 8-12

Opposite: Feta Cheese Pastries and Falafel Snacks

Pasta

Pasta is the perfect vegetarian food – healthy, filling and infinitely versatile. Not only are there so many different types and shapes of pasta, but there are also endless flavourings and delicious sauces that you can serve with it. In this chapter, you will find recipes for classic filled and baked pasta dishes, quick pasta suppers, gnocchi and polenta.

Ravioli with Sage

The best ravioli is made with home-made pasta, but if you haven't got the time or the inclination to make it yourself, you can buy some sheets of fresh ready-made lasagne from a supermarket or delicatessen and use them instead. You can use this basic recipe for pasta to make tagliatelle, lasagne, cannelloni and other types of pasta. To vary the flavour and colour of the pasta, try adding one of the following when making the dough: some finely chopped herbs; some cooked chopped spinach; or a tablespoon of tomato purée.

300 g/10 oz strong plain
bread flour
pinch of salt
3 eggs
1 tablespoon olive oil
flour for dusting
50 g/2 oz butter, melted
few fresh sage leaves, torn
grated vegetarian Parmesan cheese

FOR THE FILLING:
225 g/8 oz ricotta cheese
2 tablespoons pesto sauce
1 egg yolk
salt and freshly ground
black pepper

1 Make the pasta: sift the flour and salt into a mixing bowl. Make a well in the centre and add the eggs. Draw the flour in from the sides and mix well. Add the olive oil and continue mixing with your hands until you have a soft, pliable dough.

2 Knead the dough on a lightly floured surface for 5-10 minutes, until silky and elastic. Leave to rest in a cool place for 15 minutes.

3 Roll out the dough on a lightly floured surface, rolling and stretching it until it is really thin. Leave it for about 10 minutes to rest and dry out before using.

4 Mix all the filling ingredients together in a bowl. Cut the dough in half and trim the edges, so that you have 2 large squares. Mark one half into smaller squares and then drop teaspoonfuls of the filling into the marked squares.

5 Cover with the other sheet of pasta, and press gently around each little mound of filling with your fingertips. Cut the pasta into squares with a pastry cutter wheel.

6 Bring a large pan of lightly salted water to the boil and drop in the ravioli squares. Cook for about 5 minutes, until the ravioli rise to the surface and are tender (al dente). Remove with a slotted spoon and drain well.

7 Serve the ravioli with melted butter, sprinkled with sage, black pepper and Parmesan cheese.

Serves 4

Opposite: Ravioli with Sage

Cannelloni with Tomato Sauce

1 quantity fresh pasta (see page 30)
or 16 cannelloni tubes
75 ml/3 fl oz single cream
25 g/1 oz grated vegetarian
Parmesan cheese

FOR THE FILLING:
300 g/10 oz fresh spinach, washed
and tough stalks removed
250 g/9 oz ricotta cheese
1 teaspoon freshly grated nutmeg
salt and freshly ground black pepper
2 egg yolks

25 g/1 oz grated vegetarian
Parmesan cheese

FOR THE TOMATO SAUCE:
2 tablespoons olive oil
1 onion, finely chopped
2 garlic cloves, crushed
1 x 400-g/14-oz can chopped
tomatoes
1 teaspoon tomato purée
few basil leaves, chopped
1 teaspoon sugar
salt and freshly ground black pepper

Pasta tubes filled with spinach and ricotta make a substantial supper dish. You can use either fresh pasta or the ready-made tubes.

1 Make the tomato sauce: heat the oil and sauté the onion and garlic until soft and translucent. Add the tomatoes and tomato purée and simmer gently for 10-15 minutes, until thickened. Add the basil, sugar and salt and pepper to taste.

2 Make the filling: put the spinach leaves in a heavy-based saucepan with 1-2 tablespoons of water. Cover with a lid and cook gently over very low heat for about 5 minutes until the leaves go limp and give out their juice. Drain the spinach in a colander, pressing down well with a small plate or saucer to squeeze out any excess moisture.

3 Chop the spinach roughly and mix in a bowl with the ricotta cheese, nutmeg, seasoning, egg yolks and Parmesan cheese.

4 Cut the fresh pasta (if using) into large squares, and divide the filling between them. Roll up into cylinder shapes. Alternatively, if using ready-made cannelloni tubes, spoon the filling into the tubes.

5 Arrange the cannelloni in an oiled ovenproof dish and pour the tomato sauce over them. Drizzle the cream over the top and then sprinkle with Parmesan cheese. Bake in a preheated oven at 200°C, 400°F, Gas Mark 6 for about 20 minutes.

Serves 4

Deluxe Macaroni Cheese

50 g/2 oz butter
2 leeks, cleaned, trimmed and
sliced diagonally
2 courgettes, sliced
50 g/2 oz sun-dried tomatoes
in oil, thinly sliced
225 g/8 oz macaroni
25 g/1 oz grated
Cheddar cheese
1 tablespoon fresh white
breadcrumbs
15 g/½ oz butter
1 tablespoon chopped parsley

FOR THE SAUCE:
25 g/1 oz butter
25 g/1 oz flour
600 ml/1 pint milk
1 teaspoon Dijon mustard
good pinch of paprika
115 g/4 oz grated
Cheddar cheese
50 g/2 oz crumbled blue cheese,
e.g. Stilton
salt and freshly ground
black pepper

Here's a luxurious version of the old standby and it tastes nothing like the thick, stodgy dish beloved of school dinner ladies. This Macaroni Cheese has been tarted up by the addition of sun-dried tomatoes, leeks, courgettes and blue cheese. You could try adding sautéed mushrooms or onions to ring the changes.

1 Melt the butter and gently sauté the leeks and courgettes until softened and slightly coloured. Stir

in the sun-dried tomatoes and remove from the heat.

2 Meanwhile, cook the macaroni in a large pan of lightly salted boiling water for about 10 minutes, until tender. Drain well.

3 Make the sauce: melt the butter and stir in the flour. Cook gently for 1 minute, then gradually add the milk, stirring all the time, until the sauce is thick and smooth. Stir in the mustard, paprika and cheeses, and simmer gently for 2-3 minutes. Season to taste.

4 Mix together the cooked macaroni and vegetables and put into a buttered 1.2-litre/2-pint ovenproof dish. Pour the cheese sauce over the top. Sprinkle with the grated Cheddar cheese and breadcrumbs, and dot the top with butter.

5 Bake the Macaroni Cheese in a preheated oven at 180°C, 350°F, Gas Mark 4 for 20-30 minutes, until the top is crisp and golden brown. Sprinkle with parsley and serve immediately.

Serves 4

Spaghetti Napoletana

This is one of the simplest pasta dishes you can make – just spaghetti tossed in a fresh tomato sauce. For a stronger, more fiery flavour, add a couple of finely chopped chilli peppers and you will have an arrabbiata sauce.

---

350 g/12 oz spaghetti
50 g/2 oz grated vegetarian
Parmesan or Pecorino cheese

FOR THE SAUCE:
5 tablespoons olive oil
1 large onion, finely chopped
2 garlic cloves, crushed
450 g/1 lb plum tomatoes,
skinned and chopped
(or 450 g/1 lb passata)
2 tablespoons tomato purée
1 teaspoon sugar
115 ml/4 fl oz dry white wine
1 tablespoon finely chopped parsley
few basil leaves, torn
salt and freshly ground
black pepper
a few ripe black olives, pitted
(optional)

---

1 To make the sauce, heat the olive oil and gently fry the onion and garlic until soft and lightly coloured. Add the tomatoes, tomato puré, sugar and white wine. Simmer gently for about 15 minutes, until the tomato sauce has thickened and reduced a little. Stir in the chopped parsley and basil and season to taste with salt and pepper. Add the olives, if using.

2 While the sauce is cooking, bring a large saucepan of salted water to the boil and add the spaghetti. Boil rapidly for 8-10 minutes until the pasta is cooked and *al dente* (tender to the bite). Drain well.

3 Toss the pasta in the tomato sauce and serve immediately, sprinkled with Parmesan or Pecorino cheese. A crisp salad of bitter leaves in a mustardy vinaigrette dressing makes a good accompaniment.

Serves 4

Roasted Vegetable Lasagne

Serves 6

Use the dried lasagne sheets which do not require pre-cooking. Roasting the vegetables adds sweetness and a new dimension to this dish. If it's more convenient, you can prepare the lasagne a few hours ahead or even the previous day, and refrigerate it until you are ready to cook the meal.

10-12 sheets lasagne
1 quantity tomato sauce (see page 32)
25 g/1 oz grated vegetarian
Parmesan cheese

FOR THE ROASTED
VEGETABLES:
1 red pepper, seeded and cubed
1 green pepper, seeded and cubed
1 small aubergine, cubed
1 onion, thickly sliced and cubed
1 red onion, thickly sliced and cubed
2 courgettes, sliced

1 garlic clove, crushed
1 tablespoon chopped mixed herbs
3 tablespoons olive oil
salt and freshly ground
black pepper

FOR THE WHITE SAUCE:
25 g/1 oz butter
25 g/1 oz plain flour
600 ml/1 pint milk
pinch of grated nutmeg
salt and freshly ground
black pepper

1 Prepare the vegetables and arrange them in a roasting pan. Sprinkle with the crushed garlic and herbs and toss lightly in the olive oil. Season with salt and pepper. Cook in a preheated oven at 200°C, 400°F, Gas Mark 6 for about 30 minutes, until tender and just beginning to char.

2 Meanwhile, make the white sauce. Melt the butter and stir in the flour. Cook over low heat for 2-3 minutes, then gradually add the milk, beating well after each addition, until the sauce is thick and smooth. Season with nutmeg and salt and pepper, reduce the heat and cook gently for 2 minutes.

3 Assemble the lasagne in a large buttered ovenproof dish. Cover the base with a layer of tomato sauce and then a layer of the roasted vegetables. Cover with sheets of lasagne, and spread some white sauce over the top. Continue layering up in this way, finishing with a layer of lasagne topped with white sauce.

4 Sprinkle with Parmesan cheese and bake in a preheated oven at 190°C, 375°F, Gas Mark 5 for 20-25 minutes, until the top is crisp and golden. Cut into portions and serve with a crisp salad.

Pasta Primavera

This is a lovely 'green' dish to serve in early summer when there are so many fresh seasonal vegetables to choose from. You need not slavishly follow the recipe given here – experiment with whatever vegetables are available. Thin green beans, snow peas, mange-tout and shredded spring greens can all be added to the pasta.

1 Make the herb butter: beat the softened butter with the herbs and set aside.

300 g/10 oz fine asparagus, trimmed
and sliced diagonally
225 g/8 oz fresh peas, shelled
350 g/12 oz broad beans, shelled
4 baby courgettes, sliced diagonally
3 tablespoons fruity green olive oil
1 garlic clove, crushed
4 spring onions, roughly chopped
salt and freshly ground black pepper

450 g/1 lb angel's hair pasta
grated vegetarian Parmesan
cheese, to serve

FOR THE HERB BUTTER:
25 g/1 oz unsalted butter, softened
1 tablespoon finely chopped
parsley
1 tablespoon snipped chives

2 Blanch the asparagus, peas, broad beans and courgettes in lightly salted boiling water for 1 minute. Drain well in a colander.

3 Heat the olive oil in a large sauté pan, add the garlic and cook gently for 1-2 minutes. Add all the drained vegetables and the spring onions, and toss in the olive oil over low heat for a few minutes until they are just tender. Season to taste.

4 Meanwhile, cook the pasta in lightly salted boiling water until just tender (al dente). Drain and toss with the vegetables and herb butter. Serve at once sprinkled with a little Parmesan cheese.

Serves 4

Pasta with Mushrooms

This is an easy dish that you can rustle up in less than half an hour when you dash in from work at the end of a busy day. You can use literally any dried pasta that you can find in the larder, but the broad noodles called pappardelle are particularly good. If you don't have many fresh mushrooms, use some dried porcini.

1 Heat the olive oil and butter in a large frying pan, and stir in the mushrooms. Cook gently over low heat until the mushrooms soften and start to turn golden.

1 tablespoon olive oil
50 g/2 oz butter
450 g/ 1 lb mixed fresh mushrooms,
sliced (e.g. chestnut, morels,
chanterelles, pieds bleus,
trompettes, ceps or even button)
150 ml/5 fl oz dry white wine

115 ml/4 fl oz double cream
salt and freshly ground black pepper
300 g/10 oz dried pappardelle
or fettuccine
25 g/1 oz vegetarian Parmesan
cheese
2 tablespoons chopped parsley

2 Pour in the white wine and turn up the heat. Let the wine bubble and reduce down until it is almost syrupy. Stir in the cream and heat through gently. Season with salt and pepper.

3 Meanwhile, cook the pasta in lightly salted boiling water until it is tender (al dente). Drain well and add to the pan of mushroom sauce.

4 Toss lightly together and serve immediately, sprinkled with shavings of fresh Parmesan cheese and chopped parsley.

Serves 4

Florentine Pasta

This is the ultimate in healthy fast food – a vibrant dish that can be cooked in minutes. The rocket adds a slightly bitter touch to the creamy gorgonzola and spinach sauce.

300 g/10 oz fresh spinach
50 g/2 oz rocket
4 tablespoons milk
15 g/½ oz butter
225 g/8 oz gorgonzola, crumbled
115 ml/4 fl oz crème fraîche
salt and freshly ground black pepper
350 g/12 oz tagliatelle

1 Wash the spinach and rocket. Shake dry and remove any tough stalks. Place the spinach and rocket leaves in a large saucepan, cover with a lid and cook for 5 minutes, until they have wilted in the heat of the pan and turned bright green.

2 Drain in a colander, pressing down well with a small plate to extract any excess liquid in the spinach and rocket.

3 Put the milk, butter and crumbled gorgonzola in a small pan and stir gently over very low heat until melted and blended. Stir in the crème fraîche and season to taste. Stir in the drained spinach and rocket.

4 Meanwhile, cook the tagliatelle in lightly salted boiling water until tender (al dente). Drain and toss in the gorgonzola sauce.

Serves 4

Pasta al Pesto

If you are tempted to rush into the supermarket and buy a jar or carton of ready-made pesto sauce for this recipe, don't! Home-made pesto, using the finest ingredients, is infinitely better, fresher and a more vivid green than anything you can buy. If you can't get vegetarian Parmesan, use grano pedano or Pecorino instead.

450 g/1 lb pasta shapes
freshly ground black pepper
50 g/2 oz pine nuts
50 g/2 oz vegetarian Parmesan cheese

FOR THE PESTO SAUCE:
50 g/2 oz pine nuts

2 garlic cloves, crushed
50 g/2 oz fresh basil leaves
75 g/3 oz grated vegetarian Parmesan cheese
juice of ½ lemon
115 ml/4 fl oz olive oil

1 Make the pesto sauce: spread out the pine nuts on a baking sheet and place in a preheated oven at 220°C, 425°F, Gas Mark 7 for about 3-4 minutes, until golden brown.

2 Put the pine nuts and garlic in a blender or food processor and process to a thick paste. Add the basil leaves and process for a few seconds. Add the Parmesan cheese and lemon juice, and blend again.

3 Add the olive oil through the feed tube in a thin stream, processing all the time. You will end up with a thick green sauce.

4 Cook the pasta in lightly salted boiling water until just tender (al dente). Drain well, sprinkle with freshly ground black pepper, and toss in the pesto sauce. Stir in the pine nuts and serve, sprinkled with Parmesan cheese.

Serves 4

Spinach Gnocchi

To be successful, gnocchi must be light, not stodgy and rib sticking. Home-made taste best but you can cheat and use vacuum-packed gnocchi instead. Gnocchi can be served with pesto sauce or a simple tomato sauce, or they can be baked with cheese as in this recipe.

225 g/8 oz fresh spinach
600 g/1¼ lb floury potatoes, boiled
175 g/6 oz flour
1 egg, beaten
pinch of grated nutmeg
salt and freshly ground black pepper
175 g/6 oz gorgonzola, crumbled
150 ml/¼ pint cream

1 Wash the spinach and remove any hard stalks. Put the leaves in a large saucepan, cover with a lid and cook gently over low heat for about 5 minutes, until the leaves wilt and turn bright green. Drain in a colander and press down with a plate to squeeze out any excess water. Chop the spinach finely.

2 Mash the potatoes thoroughly to remove any lumps – ideally, pass them through a food mill. Beat in the spinach, flour, egg, nutmeg and seasoning.

3 Turn out the mixture on to a lightly floured board and knead well until the dough is soft and pliable. Then, with floured hands, roll small pieces of dough into sausage shapes, the thickness of your thumb. Press down on each one with the prongs of a fork.

4 Tip the gnocchi into a large saucepan of lightly salted boiling water and cook rapidly until they rise to the surface and float. Remove with a slotted spoon and arrange in a buttered ovenproof dish.

5 Scatter the gorgonzola over the gnocchi and pour the cream over the top. Bake in a preheated oven at 190°C, 375°F, Gas Mark 5 for 10-15 minutes until bubbling and golden.

Serves 4

Polenta with Sicilian Tomato Sauce

Traditionally polenta is peasant food – hearty and rustic. However, it has now become an elegant and fashionable dish, toasted or fried in good olive oil or butter. You can serve it either way in this recipe, soft or fried, with a piquant fresh tomato and chilli sauce. To make soft polenta decadently rich and wonderful, stir in some mascarpone, sliced

1 litre/1¾ pints water
salt
175 g/6 oz polenta
25 g/1 oz unsalted butter
olive oil or butter for frying (optional)
grated Parmesan cheese and fresh basil, to serve

FOR THE TOMATO SAUCE:
3 tablespoons olive oil

1 small onion, chopped
2 garlic cloves, crushed
1 red chilli, seeded and finely chopped
450 g/1 lb plum tomatoes, seeded and chopped
2 tablespoons capers, drained
2 tablespoons toasted pine nuts
115 g/4 oz black olives, pitted and roughly chopped
few basil leaves, torn
salt and freshly ground black pepper

Taleggio or crumbled gorgonzola cheese before serving.

1 Make the polenta: bring the water and salt to the boil in a large saucepan. Add the polenta gradually in a thin, steady stream, whisking all the time. Reduce the heat as low as it will go and continue stirring the polenta with a wooden spoon until it is thick and smooth and has absorbed all the liquid. This takes about 15-20 minutes.

2 When the polenta leaves the sides of the pan clean, stir in the butter.

You can serve the polenta like this – all fluffed up like mashed potato, adding some grated cheese and black pepper, if wished, or you can pour it into an oiled tin and leave to cool. When cold, cut into squares and fry in olive oil or butter until crisp and golden.

3 To make the tomato sauce, heat the olive oil and gently sweat the onion and garlic until soft. Add the chilli and cook for 2 minutes. Stir in the tomatoes, capers, pine nuts and olives and simmer gently, uncovered, for 30 minutes, until reduced and thickened. Stir in the torn basil leaves and season.

Polenta with Sicilian Tomato Sauce

4 Serve the sauce with the polenta, sprinkled with some freshly grated Parmesan cheese and garnish with more basil.

Serves 4

Rice, Grains, Beans & Pulses

Rice, grains, beans and pulses are all nutritious staple foods for vegetarians, being rich in protein, fibre, vitamins and minerals. Ideally, they should form an important part of your daily diet. As well as regular long-grain rice, you will discover dishes using couscous and crunchy bulgur wheat. Beans and pulses can make your diet more interesting and healthy. Try the Caribbean fritters or Mexican tacos and see for yourself.

Vegetable **Couscous**

Couscous is the fluffy grain of the Mahgreb, the countries of North Africa. Traditionally, it is steamed above a spicy bubbling stew, and red-hot harissa paste is stirred into the vegetable mixture just before serving the couscous.

3 tablespoons olive oil	600 ml/1 pint passata or sieved
1 onion, chopped	canned tomatoes
2 garlic cloves, crushed	150 ml/¹/₄ pint vegetable stock
1 aubergine, cut into	175 g/6 oz canned chick
large cubes	peas, drained
2 courgettes, cut into chunks	50 g/2 oz 'no need to soak' dried
1 red pepper, seeded and cut	apricots, sliced
into chunks	225 g/8 oz couscous
2 teaspoons ground cumin	2 teaspoons harissa paste
1 teaspoon turmeric	salt and freshly ground
1 teaspoon paprika	black pepper
¹/₂ teaspoon ground ginger	2 tablespoons chopped fresh
¹/₂ teaspoon allspice	coriander

1 Heat the olive oil in a deep saucepan and gently fry the onion and garlic until soft and golden. Add the aubergine, courgettes and red pepper and fry gently, stirring occasionally, for 5 minutes.

2 Stir in all the spices and cook gently for 1 minute. Add the passata and the stock and bring to the boil. Reduce the heat to a simmer and stir in the chick peas and apricots. Simmer for 20-25 minutes, until the vegetables are tender and the liquid has reduced.

3 About 10 minutes before serving, put the couscous in a colander lined with a J-cloth and place above the simmering vegetables.

4 Fork through the couscous to separate the grains and fluff it up. Spoon it onto the warmed serving plates. Mix the harissa paste with a little of the sauce, and either hand round separately or stir back into the vegetable stew. Check the seasoning and serve with the couscous, sprinkled with coriander.

Serves 4

Opposite: Vegetable Couscous

Rice n' Peas

This is a popular dish in Jamaica. The 'peas' are really red kidney beans. If you are in a hurry you could substitute canned kidney beans.

225 g/8 oz dried red kidney beans
1 tablespoon groundnut oil
1 onion, finely chopped
600 ml/1 pint coconut milk
300 ml/½ pint vegetable stock
2 sprigs of fresh thyme
bunch of spring onions, finely chopped
1 fresh red chilli, seeded and finely chopped
salt and freshly ground black pepper
350 g/12 oz long-grain rice
chopped coriander, to garnish

1 Put the kidney beans in a saucepan, cover with cold water and bring to the boil. Boil the beans for 10 minutes, and then remove from the heat. Set aside to soak in the cooking liquid for at least 1 hour. Drain and rinse the beans, return to the pan and cover with fresh water. Bring to the boil, then simmer gently for about 1 hour, until tender. Drain the kidney beans.

2 Meanwhile, heat the groundnut oil in another saucepan and fry the onion until soft and golden. Add the coconut milk, vegetable stock, thyme, spring onions and chilli. Season with salt and pepper and cook over medium heat for 5 minutes.

3 Tip in the rice and stir well. Cover the pan and simmer very gently for about 20 minutes until the rice is tender and all the liquid has been absorbed. Check occasionally to make sure that the rice is not sticking, and add more liquid if necessary.

4 Stir the kidney beans into the rice and sprinkle with coriander. Serve with roasted or grilled vegetables and hot pepper sauce.

Serves 4

Bulgur Wheat Pilaf

In Turkey and the Middle East, bulgur wheat is often used in pilafs in preference to rice. Its crisp, chewy texture and nutty flavour make it a delicious and nourishing grain.

4 tablespoons fruity green olive oil
1 onion, finely chopped
1 fresh red chilli, seeded and finely chopped
450 g/1 lb bulgur wheat
600 ml/1 pint boiling vegetable stock
salt and freshly ground black pepper
2 tablespoons chopped parsley or coriander

FOR THE TOPPING:
1 red pepper, seeded and chopped
1 green pepper, seeded and chopped
115 g/4 oz creamy goat's cheese or Camembert, thinly sliced

1 Heat the olive oil in a saucepan and gently fry the onion until it is soft and translucent. Add the chilli and cook for 2-3 minutes.

2 Stir in the bulgur wheat and add the boiling vegetable stock. Reduce the heat and simmer for about 20 minutes until the bulgur wheat has swelled up and absorbed the liquid. Season with salt and pepper.

3 While the pilaf is cooking, grill the peppers, turning occasionally, until the skin blackens all over. Peel the peppers, remove the seeds and cut the flesh into strips.

4 Transfer the cooked pilaf to an ovenproof dish, and arrange the peppers and sliced cheese on top. Pop under a preheated grill until the cheese starts to melt and turn golden. Serve sprinkled with chopped parsley or coriander.

Serves 4

Persian Pilaf

225 g/8 oz long-grain rice
2 tablespoons oil
1 onion, finely chopped
1 teaspoon ground turmeric
1/2 teaspoon allspice
1/2 teaspoon ground cinnamon
4 green cardamom pods
400 ml/14 fl oz vegetable stock
50 g/2 oz presoaked dried apricots, roughly chopped
salt and ground black pepper
1 tablespoon pine nuts
2 tablespoons shelled pistachios
1 tablespoon toasted flaked almonds
few coriander leaves, torn

Many of the classic rice dishes of the Middle East and North Africa are flavoured with spices and fruit. This may seem an unusual combination nowadays but they date from the Middle Ages when apricots, quinces and dates were often included in savoury dishes.

1 Tip the rice into a colander and wash thoroughly under running cold water.

2 Heat the oil in a large saucepan and fry the onion until soft and golden. Stir in all the spices and cook for 2-3 minutes until they release their aroma.

3 Stir in the rice and vegetable stock, and bring to the boil. Reduce the heat, stir in the apricots and cover the pan. Simmer gently for 15-20 minutes, until the rice has fluffed up and absorbed all the liquid.

4 Season to taste and sprinkle with the nuts before serving. If wished, scatter some torn coriander leaves over the top.

Serves 4

Vegetable Biriyani

You don't have to go out to an Indian restaurant to enjoy a spicy vegetable biriyani. All the ingredients are now available in your local supermarket.

1 Heat the ghee or oil in a large saucepan and fry the onion and garlic until soft and golden. Stir in the cloves, cardamom pods, cinnamon, chilli and ginger. Fry gently for 2-3 minutes.

2 Add the rice and cook over low heat, stirring occasionally, for 5 minutes, until all the grains are translucent and glistening.

3 Add the prepared vegetables and vegetable stock. Bring to the boil, then reduce the heat and add the remaining spices. Simmer gently for 25-30 minutes, until the vegetables are tender and the rice is cooked and

3 tablespoons ghee or vegetable oil
1 large onion, finely chopped
2 garlic cloves, crushed
6 cloves
4 green cardamom pods
1 x 2.5-cm/1-in cinnamon stick
1 fresh green chilli, finely chopped
1 x 2.5-cm/1-in piece fresh root ginger, peeled and chopped
450 g/1 lb Basmati rice
2 carrots, cubed
1 small cauliflower, divided into florets
2 courgettes, sliced thickly
75 g/3 oz okra, trimmed and sliced thickly
50 g/2 oz shelled peas
600 ml/1 pint vegetable stock
2 tablespoons ground coriander seeds
1 teaspoon ground cumin
3 tablespoons sultanas
salt and freshly ground black pepper

FOR THE GARNISH:
25 g/1 oz ghee or unsalted butter
2 large onions, sliced
25 g/1 oz blanched slivered almonds

plumped up. It should absorb all the liquid. Check the pan from time to time, adding more liquid if necessary. Stir in the sultanas and season to taste.

4 While the rice is cooking, heat the ghee or butter in a frying pan and fry the onions until they are golden brown. Remove with a slotted spoon and drain on kitchen paper.

5 Serve the biriyani sprinkled with the fried onions and almonds. A yogurt raita or tomato and coriander relish makes a good accompaniment.

Serves 4

Creole **Coconut** Rice

2 tablespoons groundnut oil
1 small onion, chopped
1 garlic clove, crushed
2 red chillies, seeded and
finely chopped
225 g/8 oz long-grain rice
600 ml/1 pint coconut milk
salt and freshly ground
black pepper
grated zest of 1 lime
1 tablespoon snipped chives
lime wedges and sprigs of
coriander, to garnish

This aromatic rice evokes the flavours and fragrances of the Caribbean. Serve it with grilled or curried vegetables, fried bananas and some West Indian hot pepper sauce.

1 Heat the oil in a deep sauté pan and gently fry the onion and garlic until golden. Add the chillies and fry for 2-3 minutes.

2 Stir in the rice and add the coconut milk. Bring to the boil, then reduce the heat and simmer very gently for 15-20 minutes, until the rice is tender and has absorbed all the liquid. Keep checking the rice while it is cooking to check that it is not sticking to the base of the pan.

3 Cover the pan with a lid and set aside to steam gently for 5 minutes. Fluff up the rice with a fork and sprinkle with the lime zest. Season to taste, scatter the chives over the top and serve garnished with lime wedges and sprigs of coriander.

Serves 4

Vegetable **Paella**

This vibrant colourful dish is familiar to anyone who has visited Spain. It should be made with Spanish Valencia rice but you could use Arborio or risotto rice instead. Many regional variations exist but rice and saffron are the two ingredients that are common to all of them. Don't leave out the saffron or use turmeric instead – there is no substitute for the real thing.

1 Heat the olive oil in a *paellera* or large shallow frying pan. Fry the onions and garlic gently until soft and golden. Add the peppers and fry for 4-5 minutes. Then add the tomatoes, beans and peas and cook for another 5 minutes.

2 Add the rice and paprika and stir

3 tablespoons fruity green
olive oil
2 onions, chopped
2 garlic cloves, crushed
1 red pepper, seeded and
sliced in rings
1 yellow pepper, seeded and
sliced in rings
450 g/1 lb tomatoes, skinned
and chopped
225 g/8 oz thin green beans,
trimmed

450 g/1 lb peas in their
pods, shelled
450 g/1 lb Valencia or
Arborio rice
1 teaspoon paprika
300 ml/$1/2$ pint dry white wine
$1/2$ teaspoon saffron
900 ml/$11/2$ pints boiling
vegetable stock
salt and freshly ground
black pepper
3 tablespoons chopped parsley

well. Pour in the white wine and bring to the boil. Mix the saffron with the boiling stock and pour into the pan. Reduce the heat a little and simmer for 5 minutes.

3 Cover the pan with a lid or some foil and place in the bottom of a preheated oven at 180°C, 350°F, Gas Mark 4 for 30-40 minutes, until the rice is tender and has absorbed all the stock. Alternatively, simmer on top of the stove in the same way as you would cook a risotto. Season to taste and stand, covered, for 5 minutes before serving sprinkled with parsley.

Serves 4-6

Opposite: Vegetable Paella

Wild mushroom risotto

Serves 4

Risotto is one of the world's most soothing, comforting dishes. It is Italian cooking at its simplest and best. The basic ingredients that are common to all risottos are butter, Arborio rice, saffron and home-made stock. To these you can add the vegetables of your choice to make an infinite variety of risottos: artichokes, asparagus, fresh herbs, mushrooms, fresh and sun-dried tomatoes or truffles.

50 g/2 oz butter
1 onion, finely chopped
350 g/12 oz risotto rice
115 ml/4 fl oz dry
white wine
450 g/1 lb wild mushrooms,
thinly sliced
1.5 litres/3 pints
boiling vegetable stock
(see page 139)

a few threads of saffron
salt and freshly ground
black pepper

TO SERVE:
15 g/½ oz butter
25 g/1 oz grated vegetarian
Parmesan cheese
3 tablespoons finely chopped
parsley

3 Add the mushrooms and stir gently until they are coated with oil.

4 Add some of the boiling stock immediately with the saffron, and cook over moderate heat, stirring from time to time. Add more stock as and when it is needed – the rice should absorb it gradually. When the rice is tender and creamy and all the stock has been absorbed, remove the pan from the heat. Season to taste and stir in the butter and Parmesan cheese. Sprinkle with parsley and serve the risotto piping hot.

1 Melt the butter in a large heavy frying pan and fry the onion until soft and golden.

2 Add the rice, stirring well with a wooden spoon until all the grains are glistening and translucent. Pour in the wine and turn up the heat. Boil rapidly until it reduces.

Butter **Beans** with Mushroom Sauce

2 x 400-g/14-oz cans butter
beans
25 g/1 oz butter
1 small onion, chopped
350 g/12 oz chestnut mushrooms,
thinly sliced
150 ml/1/4 pint white wine
or Madeira
1 tablespoon chopped tarragon
150 ml/1/4 pint double cream
pinch of grated nutmeg
1 teaspoon whole-grain
mustard
salt and freshly ground
black pepper
75 g/3 oz grated Cheddar cheese

This is a quick standby supper when you don't have time to cook a big meal. Eat it with crisp salad and some crusty or ciabatta bread. You can use dried beans soaked overnight and then cook them until tender, but canned beans are much more convenient and taste just as good.

1 Rinse the beans in a colander under running cold water, and drain well.

2 Melt the butter in a large frying pan, add the onion and cook gently until soft and translucent. Add the mushrooms and cook for about 5 minutes, until coloured.

3 Stir in the wine or Madeira and tarragon, and turn up the heat. Let it bubble until the liquid is reduced and slightly syrupy.

4 Add the cream, nutmeg and mustard and simmer gently for 2-3 minutes. Stir in the drained butter beans, and season to taste. Sprinkle the Cheddar cheese over the top and pop briefly under a preheated grill until the cheese melts and starts to bubble. Serve with a dressed salad.

Serves 4

Caribbean **Accras**

These little fritters, which are made with ground black-eyed peas, are eaten widely as an appetizer with rum punch throughout the Caribbean, especially in the French-speaking islands. If you can get them, use the red-hot Scotch bonnet chillies.

1 Put the black-eyed peas in a bowl, cover with cold water and leave to soak overnight. The following day, drain the peas and rinse them under running cold water. Rub off the skins between your fingers.

225 g/8 oz black-eyed peas
2 fresh red chillies, seeded and chopped
1 garlic clove, crushed

good pinch of salt
1-2 tablespoons milk
oil for deep-frying

2 Put the peas in a blender or food processor with the chillies, garlic and salt and process until you have a smooth, thick paste.

3 Spoon into a bowl and beat well with a wooden spoon. Beat in enough milk to make a lighter, fluffier mixture.

4 Heat the oil to 190°C, 375°F and then drop in teaspoonfuls of the mixture, a few at a time, and fry until golden brown all over. Remove with a slotted spoon, drain on kitchen paper and keep warm while you fry the remaining mixture in the same way. Serve hot. A bowl of salsa (see page 16) or mango relish goes well with the accras.

Serves 4

Spicy Dal

Dal is a vegetarian staple in India; it can be made from red split lentils, whole green lentils, moong dal or even dried beans. For speed and convenience, this recipe uses red split lentils, which are now readily available from supermarkets. Serve the dal with boiled rice or pilaf and some fresh leaf spinach and plain yogurt.

200 g/7 oz red split lentils
900 ml/1½ pints water
½ teaspoon ground turmeric
50 g/2 oz ghee or unsalted butter
1 small onion, thinly sliced
2 garlic cloves, finely chopped
1 teaspoon cumin seeds
1 teaspoon ground coriander
1 fresh green chilli, seeded and finely chopped
salt and freshly ground black pepper
2 tablespoons chopped fresh coriander

1 Put the lentils in a sieve and rinse well under running cold water. Drain and transfer to a large saucepan. Add the water and turmeric and bring to the boil. Skim any scum off the surface, then cover the pan and simmer gently for about 1-1¼ hours, until the lentils are tender and slightly mushy. Stir occasionally to prevent them sticking.

2 While the lentils are cooking, heat the ghee or butter in a frying pan and fry the onion and garlic until soft and coloured. Add the spices and chilli and cook for 2-3 minutes, until they release their aroma.

3 Stir the spicy onion mixture into the cooked lentils, season and serve sprinkled with coriander. If wished, you can beat the lentil mixture with a wooden spoon until thick and puréed, stir in the onions and serve.

Serves 4

Bean Crumble

This is a variation on the cassoulets of south-west France – haricot beans in a robust red wine sauce, topped with a savoury nutty crumble.

1 Soak the beans in cold water overnight. Drain and refresh under cold running water. Place the beans in a saucepan with the onion and bay leaf, cover with water and bring to the boil. Reduce the heat and simmer for 2 hours, until tender. Drain the beans, reserving 115 ml/4 fl oz of the cooking liquid.

2 Heat the oil in a flameproof casserole and fry the onion, garlic and carrots until soft. Stir in the remaining ingredients and bring to the boil. Reduce the heat and add the drained beans and reserved cooking

225 g/8 oz haricot beans
1 onion, studded with 3 cloves
1 bay leaf
2 tablespoons olive oil
1 large onion, chopped
1 garlic clove, crushed
2 carrots, sliced
2 tablespoons tomato purée
1 tablespoon chopped oregano and parsley
115 ml/4 fl oz red wine
4 tomatoes, skinned and chopped

1 teaspoon brown sugar
salt and freshly ground black pepper
few drops of soy sauce

FOR THE CRUMBLE:
75 g/3 oz wholemeal flour
25 g/1 oz rolled oats
salt and pepper
40 g/1½ oz butter, diced
2 tablespoons chopped Brazil nuts
3 tablespoons grated cheese

liquid. Cover and cook in a preheated oven at 180°C, 350°F, Gas Mark 4 for 30 minutes.

3 Meanwhile, make the crumble. Put the flour, oats and seasoning in a bowl and rub in the butter. Mix in the nuts and cheese.

4 After 30 minutes, remove the casserole from the oven and sprinkle the crumble over the top. Increase the oven temperature to 200°C, 400°F, Gas Mark 6 and bake, uncovered, for a further 30-40 minutes.

Serves 4

Bean Tacos

Another Mexican dish. Here, the tortillas are stuffed with a spicy bean mixture and then fried until golden and crisp. You can buy ready-made flour or corn soft tortillas in most supermarkets.

2 tablespoons olive oil
1 large onion, chopped
2 garlic cloves, crushed
2 fresh red chillies, seeded and finely chopped
1 tablespoon tomato purée
1 x 400-g/14-oz can chopped tomatoes
2 x 400-g/14-oz cans kidney beans or black beans
salt and freshly ground black pepper

2 tablespoons chopped fresh coriander
12 tortillas
oil for frying

TO SERVE:
50 g/2 oz grated Cheddar cheese
115 ml/4 fl oz soured cream
1 quantity salsa (see page 16)
guacamole (see page 141) or diced avocado

1 Heat the olive oil and fry the onion and garlic until soft and golden. Add the chillies and cook for 2-3 minutes.

2 Stir in the tomato purée and tomatoes and simmer for 10-15 minutes until the sauce reduces and thickens slightly.

3 Drain the canned beans and rinse under running cold water. Add the beans to the tomato sauce. Heat through and season to taste with salt and pepper. Stir in the coriander and remove from the heat.

4 Place a little of the tomato and bean mixture on each tortilla and roll up tightly. Secure with wooden cocktail sticks.

5 Heat the oil and fry the tacos until golden brown all over, turning occasionally. Remove and drain on kitchen paper. Sprinkle the hot tacos with Cheddar cheese and serve with soured cream, salsa and guacamole.

Serves 4

Frijoles Refritos

Otherwise known as refried beans, this is the most common way of serving beans in Mexico. The beans are cooked, then fried and mashed, and the paste is used as a filling for tortillas or served hot, garnished with guacamole, soured cream, salsa or sliced avocado.

225 g/8 oz dried pinto beans
4 garlic cloves, sliced
1 bay leaf
2 tablespoons vegetable fat or butter
1 large onion, chopped
salt and freshly ground black pepper
75 g/3 oz grated Cheddar cheese

1 Put the beans in a large bowl, cover with cold water and soak overnight. Drain the beans and rinse well under running cold water.

2 Put the beans in a large saucepan with the garlic cloves and bay leaf. Cover with plenty of cold water and bring to the boil. Reduce the heat and simmer gently for 2 hours, or until the beans are cooked and tender. Drain, reserving the cooking liquid.

3 Put the drained beans in a large bowl and mash coarsely, adding some of the reserved cooking liquid.

4 Heat the vegetable fat or butter in a large frying pan and gently fry the onion until soft and golden. Add the mashed beans, stir well and cook over low heat for a few minutes. Add some more of the cooking liquid if necessary. Season to taste with salt and pepper.

5 Serve hot, sprinkled with the grated Cheddar cheese.

Serves 4

Opposite: Bean Tacos

Provençal **Bean** Casserole

You need a strong-bodied red wine for this country-style casserole. Serve it with baked potatoes and green vegetables for a warming winter supper.

225 g/8 oz dried haricot beans
25 g/1 oz butter
2 tablespoons olive oil
1 onion, finely chopped
1 garlic clove, crushed
2 carrots, sliced
4 tomatoes, skinned and chopped
300 ml/½ pint red wine
1 bouquet garni
2 sprigs of rosemary
1 x 5-cm/2-in piece of orange rind
75 g/3 oz black olives, pitted
salt and freshly ground black pepper
3 tablespoons chopped parsley or basil

1 Soak the beans in cold water overnight. Drain and rinse under running cold water. Tip the beans into a large saucepan, cover with fresh water and bring to the boil. Reduce the heat and simmer for about 1 hour, until the beans are tender. Drain and set aside.

2 Heat the butter and olive oil in a heavy saucepan or flameproof casserole, and fry the onion, garlic and carrots until soft. Add the tomatoes, red wine, bouquet garni, rosemary and orange rind and bring to the boil. Cook over medium to high heat to reduce the liquid by half. Add the drained haricot beans and then simmer gently for 10-15 minutes.

3 Add the olives and continue cooking gently for 5 minutes. Season to taste with salt and pepper and remove the bouquet garni and rosemary sprigs. Serve sprinkled with parsley or basil.

Serves 4

Pasta and Beans

This wonderful dish of borlotti beans and pasta can be eaten as a hearty soup or, as served in Italy, as a main course with plenty of crusty bread to mop up the juices.

225 g/8 oz borlotti beans
1 carrot, sliced
1 onion, sliced
1 stick celery, sliced
1.5 litres/2½ pints vegetable stock
225 g/8 oz pasta tubes or shapes
225 g/8 oz shredded spring greens or cabbage
50 g/2 oz grated vegetarian Parmesan cheese

FOR THE TOMATO SAUCE:
3 tablespoons olive oil
1 onion, chopped
2 garlic cloves, crushed
350 g/12 oz passata (sieved tomatoes)
2 tablespoons chopped parsley
salt and freshly ground black pepper

1 Soak the beans in cold water overnight. Drain and place in a large saucepan with the carrot, onion, celery stick and stock. Bring to the boil, then reduce the heat and simmer for about 1 hour, until the beans are cooked and tender.

2 Meanwhile, make the tomato sauce. Heat the olive oil and fry the onion and garlic until soft and golden. Stir in the passata and simmer for 15-20 minutes, until thickened. Add the parsley and season to taste.

3 Remove a large ladle of beans from the pan, and purée them in a blender or food processor. Return to the other beans in the cooking liquid, and stir in the tomato sauce and pasta.

4 Simmer for 10-15 minutes, until the pasta is tender. About 5 minutes before serving, stir in the spring greens or cabbage. Check the seasoning and serve in large deep plates or bowls, sprinkled with freshly grated Parmesan cheese.

Serves 6

Mexican **Bean** Stew

225 g/8 oz dried
haricot beans
3 tablespoons vegetable oil
2 onions, chopped
1 garlic clove, crushed
2 small fresh red chillies, seeded
and finely chopped
600 g/1¼ lb pumpkin
2 fresh corn cobs
2 x 400-g/14-oz cans
chopped tomatoes
salt and freshly ground
black pepper
2 tablespoons chopped
fresh coriander
soured cream and diced avocado,
for the topping

Beans are combined with sweetcorn and pumpkin in this fiery stew. You can use almost any dried beans – kidney, haricot, black or borlotti beans are all suitable. Remember when cooking beans never to add salt to the cooking water as this will harden the beans. Always season them afterwards.

1 Put the dried haricot beans in a bowl, cover with cold water and leave to soak for several hours or overnight. The following day, drain and rinse them under running cold water. Tip the beans into a large saucepan, cover with fresh water and bring to the boil. Lower the heat and simmer for about 1 hour, until the beans are cooked and tender. Drain well, reserving the cooking liquid.

2 Heat the oil and fry the onions and garlic until soft and golden. Add the chillies and fry for 2-3 minutes.

3 Remove the rind and seeds from the pumpkin and cut the flesh into chunks. Remove the kernels from the corn cobs. Add the pumpkin and corn to the pan with the tomatoes and drained beans. Simmer gently for 20-30 minutes, adding some of the reserved cooking liquid from the beans if necessary. Season to taste.

4 Serve the Mexican Bean Stew hot, sprinkled with coriander and topped with a spoonful of soured cream and some diced avocado.

Serves 4

Creamy **Flageolet** Beans

Pale green flageolets are the most elegant and delicate of all the dried beans. If you don't have time to cook the beans and want fast food, you can always use canned ones instead.

225 g/8 oz dried flageolet
beans
25 g/1 oz butter
1 onion, finely chopped
2 garlic cloves, crushed
few sprigs of tarragon,
chopped
150 ml/¼ pint single cream or
crème fraîche
1 teaspoon Dijon mustard
salt and freshly ground black pepper
fresh tarragon leaves,
to garnish

1 Soak the beans in cold water overnight. The following day, drain and rinse under running cold water. Place in a large saucepan, cover with cold water and bring to the boil. Reduce the heat and simmer until the beans are tender. Drain well.

2 Melt the butter in a frying pan and gently fry the onion and garlic until soft and golden. Add the chopped tarragon and stir into the onion mixture with the drained beans.

3 Add the cream and Dijon mustard and turn up the heat. Just before it boils, reduce the heat and simmer for 2-3 minutes. Season to taste and serve immediately sprinkled with tarragon leaves.

Serves 4

Eggs & Cheese

Eggs and cheese have a natural affinity and are an important source of protein for most vegetarians. Most cheeses are produced using animal rennet but you can buy vegetarian alternatives, which are made with microbial enzymes. These are now stocked by many supermarkets. Always opt for free-range eggs rather than battery or barn ones.

Egg-fried **Noodles**

Egg noodles stir-fried with colourful fresh vegetables and eggs make a meal in minutes. Almost any vegetables are suitable for this dish; other suggestions include mushrooms, sliced spring onions, red and green peppers, aubergine, baby sweetcorns, mange-tout and little broccoli florets.

225 g/8 oz dried egg noodles
225 g/8 oz broccoli florets
115 g/4 oz thin asparagus, trimmed
and sliced
4 tablespoons vegetable oil
2 garlic cloves, sliced
1 shallot, chopped
1 x 2.5-cm/1-in piece fresh root
ginger, chopped
1 fresh red chilli, seeded and
finely chopped
1 small yellow pepper, seeded
and thinly sliced
grated rind and juice of $^1/_2$ lime
1 tablespoon yellow bean paste
1 teaspoon sugar
2 eggs
salt and freshly ground
black pepper
2 tablespoons chopped
fresh coriander
dark soy sauce, to serve

1 Bring a large saucepan of water to the boil and plunge the egg noodles into the boiling water. Cook for a few minutes until tender. Drain and rinse in a colander under running cold water to prevent the nooddles sticking together.

2 Cook the broccoli and the asparagus in a pan of boiling water for 2-3 minutes. Drain well.

3 Heat the vegetable oil in a wok and fry the garlic, shallot, ginger and chilli for 1-2 minutes over high heat. Add the yellow pepper and the blanched broccoli and asparagus. Stir-fry for 1 minute, then add the lime rind and juice, yellow bean paste and sugar.

4 Stir in the drained noodles and break the eggs into the wok. Stir gently for 1-2 minutes until they are soft and only just set. Season to taste with salt and pepper, then sprinkle the chopped fresh coriander over the noodle mixture and serve immediately. Hand round the dark soy sauce seperately.

Serves 4

Opposite: Egg-fried Noodles

Huevos Rancheros

This is a Mexican way of cooking eggs. As you would expect, hot chillies and tomatoes feature strongly in the recipe.

2 tablespoons oil
1 large onion, finely chopped
2 garlic cloves, crushed
1 red pepper, seeded and chopped
2 fresh green chillies, seeded and finely chopped
4 large tomatoes, seeded and chopped
2 tablespoons tomato purée
115 ml/4 fl oz vegetable stock
pinch of sugar
salt and freshly ground black pepper
4 eggs
2 tablespoons chopped fresh coriander
1 large avocado, stoned, peeled and sliced

1 Heat the oil in a saucepan and fry the onion, garlic, red pepper and chillies until soft.

2 Add the tomatoes, tomato purée, vegetable stock and sugar. Bring to the boil, then reduce the heat and simmer gently until the sauce reduces and thickens slightly. Season to taste with salt and pepper.

3 Pour the tomato sauce into an oiled ovenproof dish. Make 4 wells in the sauce with the back of a spoon, and break the eggs into the wells.

4 Bake in a preheated oven at 180°C, 350°F, Gas Mark 4 for 10-12 minutes, until the eggs are set and cooked. Serve sprinkled with chopped coriander and garnish with sliced avocado.

Serves 4

Vegetable Frittata

This aromatic Italian omelette is packed with vegetables and finished off under a hot grill. It is best served lukewarm or at room temperature, cut into wedges, with a dressed salad. As well as making a good light lunch or supper dish, it is the ideal finger food for summer picnics.

3 tablespoons olive oil
2 onions, thinly sliced
3 courgettes, thinly sliced
3 tomatoes, skinned and chopped
6 large eggs
salt and freshly ground black pepper
50 g/2 oz grated pecorino cheese
few fresh basil leaves, chopped
2 tablespoons chopped fresh parsley
25 g/1 oz butter
grated vegetarian Parmesan cheese, to serve

1 Heat the olive oil in a large frying pan, and gently fry the onions for 8-10 minutes, until softened, golden brown and almost caramelized.

2 Add the courgettes and cook for a few minutes until golden on both sides, stirring occasionally. Stir in the tomatoes and cook over moderate heat for 8-10 minutes, until the mixture is reduced and thickened.

3 Break the eggs into a large bowl with the seasoning, grated cheese and herbs. Beat with a whisk until well blended. Stir the tomato mixture into the beaten eggs and mix gently.

4 Melt the butter in a clean frying pan and when it is sizzling, pour in the omelette mixture. Reduce the heat to the barest simmer and cook the omelette until it is set and golden underneath.

5 Sprinkle with Parmesan cheese and place the pan under a preheated grill to brown the top of the omelette. Slide out on to a serving plate and serve at room temperature.

Serves 4

Stuffed **Crêpes**

115 g/4 oz flour
pinch of salt
2 eggs
300 ml/¹/₂ pint milk
butter for frying
filling of your choice
(see below)
75 g/3 oz grated Gruyère cheese

Lacy, thin crêpes, filled with a savoury mixture of vegetables and cheese, are a speciality of Brittany, France. Here is a basic recipe for the crêpes together with lots of ideas for fillings.

1 Sift the flour and salt into a bowl and make a well in the centre. Break in the eggs and a little of the milk. Beat well to make a thick batter, then gradually beat in the remaining milk until the batter is smooth. Alternatively, you can make the batter in a food processor. Leave the batter to stand for at least 30 minutes before making the crêpes.

2 Melt a little knob of butter in a small frying pan, and when it is hot and sizzling pour in 2-3 tablespoons of batter – enough to coat the base of the pan. Tilt the pan to distribute the batter evenly. Cook for 1-2 minutes until the underside of the crêpe is set and golden, then flip it over and cook the other side. Slide it out onto a warm plate, then cook the remaining crêpes in the same way.

3 Fill the crêpes with the filling of your choice and roll them up into cylinder shapes or fold over. Arrange in an ovenproof dish and sprinkle the grated cheese over the top. Bake in a preheated oven at 180°C, 350°F, Gas Mark 4 for 8-10 minutes until the cheese is golden brown and bubbling.

Serves 4

Fillings for crêpes

1 Sliced wild mushrooms sautéed in butter, then mixed with a little crème fraîche and chopped chervil and chives.

2 Sliced red and yellow peppers stewed in olive oil with chopped oregano or marjoram.

3 Ratatouille of aubergines, peppers, courgettes and tomatoes.

4 Cooked leaf spinach mixed with diced gorgonzola cheese.

5 Grilled tomatoes with goat's cheese or mozzarella.

6 Peas and asparagus in a creamy tarragon and chervil sauce.

7 Spinach and ricotta filling flavoured with nutmeg (see page 52).

8 Sliced camembert or brie and fresh cranberry sauce.

9 Caramelized onions 'stewed' in butter and white wine with plenty of chopped fresh herbs.

10 Fromage frais mixed with chopped tomato, avocado, spring onions and parsley.

11 Wilted rocket, cooked in olive oil, with sliced goat's cheese.

12 Creamy blue cheese, sliced apple and toasted walnuts.

Quick **Welsh Rabbit**

4 slices bread, toasted
2 heaped tablespoons fruity chutney
225 g/8 oz grated Cheddar cheese
1 tablespoon mustard
25 g/1 oz butter, softened
2-3 tablespoons beer
few drops of Worcestershire sauce

You can use virtually any cheese, but the strongly flavoured British ones are best, e.g. a mature Cheddar or Wensleydale.

1 Spread the toast with the chutney. Mix the grated cheese with the mustard and butter and then stir in the beer and a few drops of Worcestershire sauce. Spread over the chutney.

2 Pop the toasts under a preheated hot grill, until they are golden brown and bubbling. Eat immediately as a snack.

Serves 4

Green vegetable soufflé

Serves 4

A soufflé is always a spectacular creation which inspires admiration. Instead of making a mundane cheese soufflé, why not try this light-as-air vegetable soufflé, flecked with green spinach, courgettes and broccoli? Other puréed vegetables, such as onions, asparagus, cauliflower, parsnips or even Brussels sprouts, are also suitable. Experiment with different cheeses – vegetarian Parmesan, Cheddar, Gruyère and even crumbled goat's cheese – to vary the flavour.

450 g/1 lb fresh spinach, courgettes
and broccoli
40 g/1¹/₂ oz butter
25 g/1 oz flour
150 ml/¹/₄ pint hot milk
¹/₂ teaspoon grated nutmeg

4 x size 1 eggs, separated, plus
1 egg white
50 g/2 oz grated Gruyère cheese
salt and freshly ground black pepper
2 tablespoons finely grated
vegetarian Parmesan cheese

1 Wash the fresh spinach leaves thoroughly and remove any hard stems. Trim the courgettes and slice them. Trim the stalks of the broccoli. Tip all the prepared vegetables into a large saucepan of boiling lightly salted water and cook until tender. Drain well and then purée until smooth in a food processor.

2 Melt the butter in a medium-sized saucepan and stir in the flour. Cook for 1 minute without colouring, and then beat in the hot milk, a little at a time, until thick, glossy and smooth.

Remove the pan from the heat and stir in the nutmeg. Beat in the egg yolks, one at a time, and then stir in the puréed vegetables and Gruyère. Season with plenty of salt and pepper.

3 Beat the egg whites in a clean dry bowl with a clean whisk, until they are glossy and stand up in stiff peaks when you lift out the whisk. Beat one tablespoonful of the beaten egg whites into the cheese and vegetable mixture to slacken it. Fold in the remaining egg whites gently with a metal spoon. Don't get carried away and start mixing or beating – just fold

in a gentle figure-of-eight lifting and turning movement. It does not matter if you can still see the egg white and it doesn't look uniformly green.

4 Butter a 1.5-litre/2¹/₂-pint soufflé dish generously and sprinkle the base and round the sides with a little of the grated Parmesan cheese. Pour the soufflé mixture into the dish and then sprinkle with the remaining Parmesan. Stand the dish on a hot baking sheet and bake in a preheated oven at 190°C, 375°F, Gas Mark 5 for about 30 minutes, until well-risen and golden brown on top. The crust should move only slightly; if it wobbles, return to the oven for a few more minutes. Do not open the oven door for at least 20 minutes to check how it is getting on! And be careful not to overcook it. Serve immediately.

Italian **Taleggio** Pie

This is immensely rich but a little goes a long way and it is heaven when served with a lightly dressed salad of bitter chicory, radicchio, frisée and rocket. If you can't find any Taleggio, use Brie, Camembert or even a soft, creamy goat's cheese.

350 g/12 oz puff pastry, fresh or frozen and thawed
450 g/1 lb square piece of Taleggio with rind left on
beaten egg, for glazing

1 Roll out the pastry thinly on a lightly floured surface. Cut out 2 large squares, 5 cm/2 in bigger than the piece of Taleggio.

2 Place the cheese on top of one square, and brush the edges with beaten egg. Cover with the remaining sheet of pastry and seal and decorate the edges. Place on a greased baking sheet, cut a small hole in the top and brush with beaten egg. If wished, you can decorate the pie with leaves made from the pastry trimmings.

3 If you have time, chill the pie for 15-20 minutes before baking. Bake in a preheated hot oven at 200°C, 400°F, Gas Mark 6 for 15-20 minutes, until the pastry is well-risen and golden. Resist the temptation to eat the pie immediately and let it cool a little – just 5-10 minutes – before serving with a crisp salad.

Serves 4

Gougère Puff

You rarely encounter this puffed-up savoury dish outside of France, but it's well worth making. Basically, it's just a cheesey choux pastry, and it is usually served with an aperitif before the meal. However, if you bake it in a ring and then fill the centre with a vegetable filling of your choice, it makes a good main course. Gougère is usually made with Gruyère, but a mature Cheddar or even blue-veined Stilton or Roquefort are equally delicious.

75 g/3 oz unsalted butter
200 ml/7 fl oz water
115 g/4 oz plain flour, sifted
3 large eggs, beaten
115 g/4 oz grated Gruyère cheese
salt and freshly ground black pepper
pinch of cayenne pepper

1 Put the butter and water in a saucepan and bring to a full, rolling boil. Tip in the flour immediately and remove the pan from the heat. Beat vigorously with a wooden spoon until the mixture forms a ball and leaves the sides of the pan clean.

2 Add the beaten eggs, a little at a time, beating well between each addition. You should end up with a glossy paste. Beat in 75 g/3 oz of the grated cheese, and season the mixture with salt, pepper and cayenne.

3 Drop tablespoonfuls of the cheese mixture in a circle, but not quite touching, on to a well-buttered baking tray. Sprinkle with the remaining grated Gruyère cheese.

4 Bake in a preheated oven at 220°C, 425°F, Gas Mark 7 for 25-30 minutes, until puffed up, crisp and golden brown. Cool for a few minutes before serving with drinks or a salad. Alternatively, spoon one of the suggested fillings below into the centre of the cheese ring.

Serves 4

Fillings

1 Ratatouille flavoured with fresh herbs, e.g. oregano, basil and flat-leaf parsley.

2 Sautéed chestnut or wild mushrooms in a creamy white wine sauce.

3 Butter beans in a cream sauce flavoured with whole-grain mustard and tarragon.

4 A hot salad of grilled peppers, avocado and mozzarella in garlic-scented olive oil.

5 Pumpkin, sweetcorn and red onions in a fresh tomato sauce.

Scrambled Egg Supper

When you're in a hurry and in need of comfort food, nothing beats creamy scrambled eggs. These are flavoured with chives and little pockets of cream cheese.

1 Break the eggs into a bowl and beat with a fork. Stir in the chives and some salt and pepper.

2 Melt the butter in a large non-stick frying pan over moderate heat. Pour in the egg mixture, then reduce the heat and stir with a wooden spoon until the eggs are creamy and almost set.

3 Gently fold in the chilled cubes of

8 large eggs
2 tablespoons snipped chives
salt and freshly ground black pepper
3 tablespoons butter
225 g/8 oz chilled cream cheese, diced
4 English muffins

cream cheese, taking care not to break them. Stir gently for 1 minute, until the eggs are set.

4 Meanwhile, split and toast the muffins. Serve the scrambled eggs piled on to the muffins.

Serves 4

Flavourings

You can add any of the following flavourings to scrambled eggs:

1 Diced fried mushrooms and chopped parsley.

2 Chopped watercress and whole-grain mustard.

3 Finely chopped red Thai chillies and coriander leaves.

4 Diced tomato and chopped basil leaves.

5 Grated cheese and chopped fresh tarragon.

Glamorgan Cheese Sausages

175 g/6 oz fresh white breadcrumbs
115 g/4 oz grated Caerphilly cheese
3 spring onions, finely chopped
1 teaspoon dried mixed herbs
2 tablespoons finely chopped parsley
good pinch of nutmeg
salt and freshly ground black pepper
1 large egg, beaten

FOR COATING AND FRYING:
1 egg white, lightly beaten
3-4 tablespoons flour
pinch of mustard powder
15 g/½ oz grated vegetarian Parmesan cheese
oil for shallow-frying

These delicious vegetarian 'sausages' can be made with almost any cheese but a salty Caerphilly is best. Serve them with a dollop of apple herb jelly and a mustardy watercress salad with sliced apple and walnuts.

1 Put the breadcrumbs, grated cheese, spring onions, herbs and nutmeg in a bowl and mix well together. Season with salt and pepper and then stir in the beaten egg to bind the mixture together. If it is still very stiff or a little dry, moisten with a little milk.

2 Divide the mixture into 8 or 12 portions and roll each one up between your hands into a 'sausage' shape.

3 Dip the 'sausages' in the beaten egg white and then roll them in the flour, mustard powder and Parmesan cheese.

4 Heat the oil in a frying pan and fry the 'sausages' over moderate heat, turning occasionally, until they are uniformly golden brown. Remove and drain on kitchen paper, then serve hot with salad.

Serves 4

Red-hot **Quesadillas**

12 fresh corn or wheat tortillas
175 g/ 6 oz refried beans
(see page 50)
225 g/8 oz Cheddar or Monterey
Jack cheese, grated
115 g/4 oz Mozzarella cheese, diced
2 fresh green chillies, seeded
and finely chopped
1 tablespoon finely chopped
fresh coriander
oil for frying

TO SERVE:
sea salt, salsa, guacamole, soured
cream and lime wedges

Fried tortilla parcels oozing with melted cheese are widely eaten throughout Mexico and south-west America as a snack or first course. Serve with bowls of salsa, guacamole and soured cream.

1 Spread out the tortillas and place a spoonful of refried beans on each one. Cover with grated cheese and diced Mozzarella, and scatter chillies and coriander over the top.

2 Dampen the edges of the tortillas and fold them over to cover the filling. Press the edges together firmly between your fingers and thumb. To be on the safe side, you can secure the tortillas with wooden cocktail sticks to prevent them bursting open during cooking.

3 Heat the oil in a large frying pan – it should be about 2.5 cm/1 in deep. Fry the quesadillas, a few at a time, until golden brown on both sides. Remove and drain on kitchen paper. Serve hot with sea salt, salsa, guacamole, soured cream and wedges of fresh lime.

Serves 4

Savoury **Cheese** Strudel

This is an unusual savoury version of the more familiar sweet strudel. Vegetable and cheese strudels are eaten in Eastern Europe, served with soured cream and sprinkled with paprika or caraway seeds.

25 g/ 1 oz butter
2 tablespoons olive oil
225 g/8 oz slim leeks, washed,
trimmed and sliced
115 g/4 oz mushrooms, sliced (wild
or chestnut)
225 g/8 oz shredded cabbage
1 dessert apple, peeled, cored
and sliced
1 tablespoon cider vinegar
75 ml/3 fl oz dry cider
300 g/10 oz creamy goat's
cheese, diced
150 ml/1/4 pint soured cream
2 tablespoons chopped parsley
salt and freshly ground black pepper
6 sheets of filo pastry
75 g/3 oz butter, melted

1 Heat the butter and olive oil in a large saucepan and fry the leeks until golden brown. Add the mushrooms and fry gently for 4-5 minutes until golden. Stir in the cabbage and apple and cook gently over low heat for 2-3 minutes until tender. Remove from the pan and keep warm.

2 Pour the cider vinegar and cider into the pan, stir well to loosen any residue from the base of the pan, and turn up the heat. Bubble rapidly until the liquid reduces and starts to go syrupy. Stir in the goat's cheese and soured cream and lower the heat to a simmer. Cook gently for 2-3 minutes until the cheese melts into the cream, and then stir in the cooked vegetables, parsley and seasoning.

3 Spread out 2 sheets of filo pastry, overlapping each other slightly to make a larger sheet, and brush with plenty of melted butter. Cover with half of the vegetable mixture. Cover with 2 more sheets of filo, brush with more butter and then spoon over the remaining vegetable mixture. Top with the last 2 filo sheets and brush with butter.

4 Carefully roll the pastry over lengthways, as you would a Swiss roll. Seal the ends as best you can, and place the strudel on a buttered baking sheet. Brush with any remaining melted butter and bake in a preheated oven at 190°C, 375°F, Gas Mark 5 for 20-30 minutes until the pastry is crisp and golden brown. Serve sliced with salad.

Serves 4

Opposite: Red-hot Quesadillas

Main vegetable dishes

In the following pages, you will find some new, innovative vegetable dishes as well as some old favourites, such as nut roast and moussaka, which have been enhanced with aromatic spices and elegant sauces to make them even more delicious. This is a truly international section featuring some of the world's best-loved vegetarian food.

Mediterranean Vegetable **Kebabs**

These kebabs can be cooked under a hot grill or over hot coals. The vegetables are threaded on to skewers with cubes of halloumi cheese. This is ideal for grilling because it is very firm and does not ooze under the hot grill.

2 aubergines, cut into large cubes
1 red pepper, seeded and cut into squares
1 yellow pepper, seeded and cut into squares
3 courgettes, cut into thick slices
3 small red onions, cut into quarters
450 g/1 lb halloumi cheese, cubed
2 tablespoons finely chopped flat-leaf parsley

FOR THE MARINADE:
6 tablespoons fruity green olive oil
1 garlic clove, crushed
juice of 1 lemon
1 fresh red chilli, seeded and chopped (optional)
salt and freshly ground black pepper

1 Prepare all the vegetables and place them in a large dish with the cubed halloumi cheese.

2 Mix the marinade ingredients together and then pour over the vegetables and cheese, turning them gently in the marinade. Cover and leave in a cool place for several hours or overnight if wished.

3 Thread the vegetables and cheese alternately on to 4 long kebab skewers. Cook under a preheated hot grill or over hot coals, turning occasionally, for 6-8 minutes. The vegetables should still be juicy and only slightly charred – not burnt offerings. While they are cooking, brush them frequently with the marinade to keep them moist.

4 Serve the kebabs, sprinkled with chopped parsley, with some plain boiled rice or pilaf, and a crisp salad. Salsa (see page 16) or vegetable purées (e.g. carrot or fresh pea) are also good with these kebabs.

Serves 4

Opposite: Mediterranean Vegetable Kebabs

Vegetable **Moussaka**

2 aubergines, sliced
450 g/1 lb courgettes, sliced
lengthways
4 tablespoons olive oil
15 g/½ oz butter
25 g/1 oz grated Gruyère or
vegetarian Parmesan cheese

FOR THE TOMATO AND
BEAN SAUCE:
115 g/4 oz black-eyed beans
2 tablespoons olive oil
2 onions, chopped
1 garlic clove, crushed
1 x 400-g/14-oz can
chopped tomatoes
150 ml/¼ pint white wine
1 teaspoon oregano
pinch each of ground cinnamon
and allspice
1 tablespoon chopped parsley
salt and freshly ground black pepper

FOR THE BÉCHAMEL SAUCE:
40 g/1½ oz butter
40 g/1½ oz flour
450 ml/¾ pint milk
salt and freshly ground black pepper
2 egg yolks
25 g/1 oz grated Gruyère or
vegetarian Parmesan cheese

In some parts of Greece, moussaka is made with courgettes as well as aubergines. In this version, they are layered with beans in tomato sauce and a béchamel sauce, then served with salad and pitta bread.

1 Prepare the beans for the tomato and bean sauce. Soak the black-eyed beans in cold water for 1 hour. Drain well. Place in a pan, cover with fresh water and cook for 30 minutes, until tender. Drain.

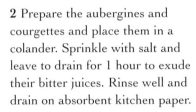

2 Prepare the aubergines and courgettes and place them in a colander. Sprinkle with salt and leave to drain for 1 hour to exude their bitter juices. Rinse well and drain on absorbent kitchen paper.

3 Meanwhile, heat the oil for the sauce in a saucepan and fry the onions and garlic until soft and golden. Add the tomatoes, wine, oregano and spices, and bring to the boil. Reduce the heat and simmer for 15-20 minutes, until reduced and thickened. Stir in the cooked beans and parsley, and season to taste.

4 While the sauce is cooking, fry the aubergines and courgettes in the olive oil and butter until they are golden on both sides. Drain well on absorbent kitchen paper.

5 Make the béchamel sauce: melt the butter over low heat and stir in the flour. Cook for 1 minute without colouring, then gradually add the milk, a little at a time, beating well after each addition, until the sauce is thick and smooth. Remove from the heat, season to taste and stir in the egg yolks and grated cheese.

6 Now it's time to assemble the moussaka. Arrange a layer of aubergines and courgettes in the base of an ovenproof dish. Cover with a layer of tomato and bean sauce. Continue layering up in this way, finishing with a layer of vegetables. Pour the thick béchamel sauce over the top and then sprinkle with grated cheese.

7 Bake the moussaka in a preheated oven at 180°C, 350°F, Gas Mark 4 for 1 hour. Remove and let it stand for 5 minutes before serving.

Serves 4

Vegetable **Tempura**

800 g/1³/₄ lb mixed vegetables, e.g.
broccoli florets, courgette batons,
button mushrooms, sliced red,
green and yellow peppers,
trimmed spring onions,
baby sweetcorn
oil for deep-frying
lemon wedges, to garnish
dark soy sauce

FOR THE BATTER:
1 large egg
225 ml/8 fl oz chilled water
150 g/5 oz plain flour
¹/₂ teaspoon salt

In Japan, vegetables are deep-fried in the lightest of batters until crisp and golden. Don't worry if some of the batter disappears into the oil. Some will end up clinging to the vegetables and the little fritters will look all the more colourful for it.

1 Make the batter. It is important to use chilled water and an egg straight from the refrigerator. Put the egg and water in a bowl with the flour and salt. Whisk quickly together – do not over-beat the batter.

2 Dip the vegetables into the batter and then deep-fry, a few at a time, in oil heated to 190°C, 375°F, until they are crisp and golden all over.

Remove the vegetables carefully with a slotted spoon and drain on absorbent kitchen paper. Fry the remaining vegetables in the same way.

3 Serve the vegetables with plain rice, garnished with lemon wedges. If wished, you can sprinkle a little soy sauce over them.

Serves 4

Pumpkin Curry

Make this curry in the autumn when fresh pumpkins are plentiful. In St Lucia it is served with rice, fried plantains and the ubiquitous hot pepper sauce. However, exotic fruit salsa (see page 140) also makes a very good accompaniment. If you can't get a fresh coconut, you could use coconut milk instead.

115 g/4 oz fresh coconut,
grated
300 ml/¹/₂ pint coconut water (from
a fresh coconut)
2 tablespoons vegetable oil
1 large onion, chopped
1 green pepper, seeded
and chopped
4 garlic cloves, crushed
1 x 2.5-cm/1-in piece fresh root
ginger, peeled and chopped

2 fresh green chillies, seeded
and finely chopped
1 tablespoon turmeric
¹/₄ teaspoon ground cloves
900 g/2 lb pumpkin, diced
2 tomatoes, skinned
and chopped
salt and freshly ground
black pepper
fresh coriander leaves,
to garnish

1 Put the grated fresh coconut in a bowl. To get the coconut water, pierce a fresh coconut with a skewer and drain out the liquid through the hole. Pour over the grated coconut and set aside for 30 minutes.

2 Heat the oil and gently fry the onion, green pepper and garlic over low heat until the onion is soft and golden brown. Stir in the ginger,

chillies, turmeric and cloves, and cook for 2-3 minutes so that the spices release their aroma.

3 Add the pumpkin, tomatoes and coconut water. Bring to the boil, then reduce the heat and simmer for 20 minutes. The curry is ready when the pumpkin is tender and just starting to disintegrate – it should not be allowed to over-cook

and go mushy. Season to taste and garnish with coriander leaves.

4 Serve the curry immediately with boiled rice. In the West Indies, some local hot pepper sauce would be stirred into the pumpkin mixture to make it even hotter. You can buy this in supermarkets.

Serves 4

Vegetable Korma

Serve this creamy curry with naan bread or boiled rice scattered with cardamoms and golden-brown fried onions. Mango chutney and banana raita would add the finishing touches to a delicately spicy meal.

50 g/2 oz ghee or unsalted butter
2 onions, sliced
2 garlic cloves, crushed
1 fresh red chilli, seeded and chopped
2.5-cm/1-in piece fresh root ginger, peeled and chopped
1 teaspoon turmeric
3 potatoes, peeled and cubed
115 g/4 oz button mushrooms
1 large aubergine, cubed
115 g/4 oz cauliflower florets
300 ml/1/2 pint water or vegetable stock
115 g/4 oz broccoli florets

150 ml/1/4 pint double cream
150 ml/1/4 pint natural yogurt
salt and freshly ground black pepper
2 tablespoons chopped coriander leaves
50 g/2 oz roasted cashew nuts

FOR THE GROUND SPICES:
2 tablespoons coriander seeds
2 tablespoons cumin seeds
1 tablespoon cardamom seeds (from green pods)
1 teaspoon mustard seeds
6 whole cloves

1 Grind the whole spices in the traditional way with a pestle and mortar, or in an electric grinder.

2 Heat the ghee or butter in a deep saucepan and fry the onions and garlic until soft and golden. Add the chilli and ginger and continue cooking over low heat for 2-3 minutes.

3 Stir in the ground spices and turmeric, and cook for 2 minutes. Then add the potatoes, mushrooms, aubergine and cauliflower. Turn quickly in the spicy mixture and then pour in the water or stock. Cover the pan and simmer gently for 15-20 minutes, until the vegetables are cooked and just tender.

4 Cook the broccoli separately in boiling salted water until just tender and still bright green. Stir into the pan with the cream and yogurt and cook very gently without boiling for 4-5 minutes. The korma will curdle if you allow it to boil!

5 Check the seasoning, adding salt and pepper to taste if needed. Serve the korma immediately, sprinkled with chopped coriander and whole roasted cashews.

Serves 4

Vegetable Fajitas

This is the ideal quick supper when you are in a hurry with little time to cook. Keep a packet of tortillas in the freezer for such occasions.

2 onions, thinly sliced
1 garlic clove, crushed
2 tablespoons olive oil
2 red peppers, seeded and sliced
1 green pepper, seeded and sliced
1 yellow pepper, seeded and sliced
2 fresh red chillies, seeded and chopped
225 g/8 oz button mushrooms, sliced

salt and freshly ground black pepper
2 tablespoons finely chopped coriander

FOR SERVING:
12 warmed tortillas
salsa (see page 16), soured cream and guacamole
sprigs of fresh coriander

1 Sauté the onions and garlic in the olive oil until soft and golden brown. Add the sliced peppers and chillies, and continue cooking until tender.

2 Add the mushrooms, turn up the heat and cook for 1 minute. Season with salt and pepper and sprinkle with chopped coriander.

3 Put a large spoonful of the sizzling vegetables on each warmed tortilla and roll up. Serve the fajitas immediately with bowls of salsa, soured cream and guacamole, garnished with sprigs of fresh coriander.

Serves: 4

Opposite: Vegetable Fajitas

Mushroom Stroganov

25 g/1 oz butter
1 onion, finely chopped
450 g/1 lb mushrooms, sliced
1-2 tablespoons brandy
300 ml/1/2 pint soured cream
pinch each of ground nutmeg
and mace
salt and ground black pepper
2 tablespoons snipped chives

FOR THE NOODLES:
350 g/12 oz tagliatelle or fettuccine
15 g/1/2 oz melted butter
1 teaspoon caraway or
poppy seeds

Mushrooms are delicious served this way in a soured cream sauce with buttered noodles. Although button mushrooms will do, field mushrooms are better, and wild mushrooms will be truly special.

1 Melt the butter in a large frying pan and sauté the onion until soft and faintly golden. Add the mushrooms and fry for 4-5 minutes, until coloured.

2 Stir in the brandy and bubble up for a few minutes until the liquid in the pan evaporates. Stir in the soured cream and spices, and simmer gently for 5 minutes, until the sauce thickens slightly. Season to taste with salt and plenty of black pepper.

3 Meanwhile, cook the noodles in lightly salted boiling water until tender. Drain well, return to the pan and toss in the melted butter and caraway or poppy seeds.

4 Sprinkle the mushroom stroganov with chives, and serve immediately with the buttered noodles and a crisp green salad.

Serves 4

Vegetable Satay

You can make a wonderful satay with grilled spicy vegetables threaded on to small wooden skewers. Serve it with cubes of lontong rice. To make this, cook boil-in-the-bag rice for about 1 hour and then leave to cool until the rice goes solid. Remove from the bag and cut into cubes. Reheat the rice cubes before serving.

2 aubergines, cut into chunks
2 small onions, cut into chunks
175 g/6 oz button mushrooms
2 green peppers, seeded and cut
into chunks
1 yellow pepper, seeded and
cut into chunks
rice and cucumber
chunks, to serve
coriander leaves, to garnish

FOR THE MARINADE:
2 garlic cloves, crushed
1 tablespoon sesame oil

3 tablespoons soy sauce
1/2 teaspoon each ground ginger
and coriander
1 tablespoon lime juice
1 teaspoon brown sugar

FOR THE SATAY SAUCE:
50 g/2 oz roasted unsalted peanuts
1/2 teaspoon salt
300 ml/1/2 pint coconut milk
1-2 teaspoons curry paste
1 tablespoon brown sugar
juice of 1/2 lime
good pinch of chilli powder

1 Prepare the aubergines, onions, mushrooms and peppers, and place in a bowl. Mix all the marinade ingredients together and spoon over the vegetables. Leave to marinate in a cool place for at least 1 hour.

2 Meanwhile, make the satay sauce. Using a pestle and mortar, grind the peanuts and salt to a thick, creamy consistency. Pour half of the coconut milk into a saucepan, stir in the curry paste, and stir over low heat

for 2-3 minutes. Add the creamed peanut mixture, sugar, lime juice, chilli powder and remaining coconut milk. Stir well, then simmer for about 15-20 minutes, until thickened.

3 Thread the marinated vegetables on to oiled wooden or bamboo skewers, and cook under a hot grill or over hot coals, turning frequently, for 6-8 minutes, until tender and ever so slightly charred. Brush them occasionally with the marinade to keep them moist.

4 Serve the vegetable skewers immediately with the satay dipping sauce, with either boiled or lontong rice and chunks of fresh cucumber. Garnish with fresh coriander leaves.

Serves 4

Sesame Pancakes

You can prepare the pancakes in advance and reheat them later just before serving. You don't have to stick to the stir-fried vegetables in the recipe. Just add whatever you have lurking in the refrigerator.

1 tablespoon sesame oil
1 fresh red chilli, seeded and finely chopped
1 x 2.5-cm/1-in piece fresh root ginger, peeled and chopped
1 bunch spring onions, trimmed and sliced diagonally
1 yellow pepper, seeded and thinly sliced
1 green pepper, seeded and thinly sliced
75 g/3 oz parboiled baby sweetcorn
75 g/3 oz parboiled thin green beans
75 g/3 oz parboiled baby asparagus
pinch of five-spice powder
2 tablespoons soy sauce
1 tablespoon dry sherry
salt and freshly ground black pepper
1 tablespoon chopped coriander leaves

FOR THE PANCAKES:
115 g/4 oz plain flour
pinch of salt
1 egg
300 ml/½ pint milk
oil for frying
2 tablespoons sesame seeds

1 Make the pancake batter: sift the flour and salt into a bowl and mix in the egg and a little of the milk. Gradually whisk in the remaining milk until you have a smooth batter. Leave to stand for 30 minutes before making the pancakes.

2 Heat a few drops of oil in a small frying pan, and when it is really hot, pour in a little of the batter, tilting the pan to cover the base. Sprinkle with a few of the sesame seeds, and when the underside of the pancake is set and golden, flip it over and cook the other side. Slide out of the pan and keep warm. Cook the remaining pancakes in the same way.

3 Cover the pancakes in foil and keep them warm while you stir-fry the vegetables for the filling.

4 Heat the sesame oil in a wok or heavy frying pan. Add the chilli and ginger and stir-fry over medium heat for 1-2 minutes. Add the spring onions and peppers, and stir-fry for 2-3 minutes. Stir in the parboiled vegetables and stir-fry for 1 minute.

5 Stir in the five-spice powder and then pour in the soy sauce and

Other pancake fillings

1 Diced creamy blue cheese, e.g. gorgonzola, with wilted rocket and chopped toasted walnuts.

2 Sliced onions, fried slowly in butter until caramelized, and chopped parsley.

3 Button mushrooms in a herb-flecked creamy sauce.

4 Strips of red and yellow peppers sautéed in olive oil, with black olives, feta cheese and herbs.

sherry. Stir-fry over high heat for 2 minutes, until the liquid evaporates. Season to taste with salt and pepper.

6 Place some of the stir-fried vegetables on each pancake and fold over or roll up. Serve immediately sprinkled with chopped coriander.

Serves 4

Spring rolls

Serves 4

A quick and easy way to make vegetable spring rolls is to use filo pastry rather than the usual wonton wrappers. The quantities are sufficient to make eight spring rolls for a main course, or twenty-four small bite-sized ones for passing round with pre-dinner drinks. If wished, you can prepare the spring rolls in advance and leave them in the refrigerator for a few hours before oiling and cooking them.

350 g/12 oz filo pastry
vegetable oil for brushing
spring onion tassels, to garnish
plum sauce or chilli sauce,
for dipping

FOR THE FILLING:
2 tablespoons sesame oil
6 spring onions, sliced diagonally
2 garlic cloves, crushed
1-2 fresh red chilli(es), seeded and
finely chopped

1 x 2.5-cm/1-in piece fresh root
ginger, peeled and chopped
2 carrots, grated
115 g/4 oz shredded
Chinese leaves
115 g/4 oz bean sprouts
75 g/3 oz mushrooms, chopped
2 tablespoons soy sauce
1 tablespoon dry sherry
pinch of sugar
1 tablespoon chopped parsley or
coriander leaves

1 Make the filling for the spring rolls. Heat the sesame oil in a wok and stir-fry the spring onions, garlic, chilli(es) and ginger for 2 minutes. Add the carrots, Chinese leaves, bean sprouts and mushrooms, and stir-fry for 2 minutes.

2 Add the soy sauce, sherry and sugar and toss the vegetables in this mixture. Turn up the heat so that the liquid almost evaporates. Remove from the heat and leave to cool. Stir in the parsley or coriander.

3 Unwrap the filo pastry, spread out one sheet and brush with oil – cover the remaining sheets with a damp cloth to prevent them drying out.

Cut the filo sheet in half and arrange some of the cooled vegetable filling along one side in a sausage shape. Turn the sides in over the edges of the filling and roll up to make a neat parcel. Assemble the other spring rolls in the same way.

4 Place the spring rolls on an oiled baking sheet, brush with oil and cook in a preheated oven at 225°C, 425°F, Gas Mark 7 for 12-15 minutes, until crisp and golden brown. Turn them over halfway through the cooking time. Serve the hot spring rolls immediately with spring onion tassels and a plum or chilli dipping sauce.

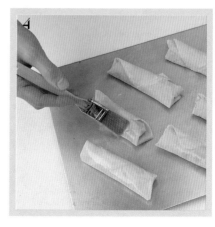

Fritto **Misto**

1 kg/2 lb prepared raw
vegetables, e.g. small fresh
artichokes, sliced aubergines,
courgette batons, radicchio
quarters, mushrooms, or
blanched vegetables, e.g.
asparagus stalks, cauliflower
and broccoli florets, sliced
fennel and celeriac
oil for deep-frying
ground sea salt
lemon wedges, to serve

FOR THE BATTER:
115 g/4 oz plain flour
pinch of salt
1 tablespoon olive oil
200 ml/7 fl oz water

An Italian *fritto misto* of mixed fried vegetables in a really crisp, light batter makes a memorable meal. You can use so many Mediterranean and seasonal vegetables, but the greatest delicacy of all, if you can get them, are orange courgette blossoms. Serve the vegetable fritters with lemon wedges and a fresh tomato sauce, or a simple bowl of fromage frais into which you have stirred some red or green pesto sauce.

1 Make the batter: sift the flour and salt into a mixing bowl and make a well in the centre. Mix in the olive oil and beat in the water. Beat well with a wooden spoon to make a smooth batter. Leave to stand for about 1 hour before using.

2 Prepare all the vegetables. Wash the raw ones, pat dry and leave whole, or cut or slice into smaller portions. Blanch the other vegetables in boiling water, then drain well and dry on absorbent kitchen paper.

3 Dip the vegetables quickly into the prepared batter and shake off any excess batter. Deep-fry in oil heated to 190°C, 375°F for a few minutes, until crisp and golden. Remove with a slotted spoon, drain on kitchen paper and serve immediately, sprinkled with salt, with lemon wedges. A crisp salad of radicchio and bitter leaves tossed in a lemony olive oil dressing is the perfect accompaniment.

Serves 4

Layered **Nut** Roast

1 onion, finely chopped
2 garlic cloves, crushed
50 g/2 oz butter
175 g/6 oz brazil nuts,
ground
50 g/2 oz hazelnuts, ground
175 g/6 oz shelled chestnuts, roughly
chopped
50 g/2 oz wholemeal
breadcrumbs
225 g/8 oz mashed
cooked swede
2 tablespoons chopped
fresh parsley
1 teaspoon chopped
fresh oregano
1 teaspoon fresh thyme leaves

1/2 teaspoon cayenne pepper
1 tablespoon mixed
nut butter (almonds,
hazelnuts, cashews)
grated rind and juice of 1 lemon
1 egg, beaten
50 ml/2 fl oz vegetable stock
salt and freshly ground
black pepper

FOR THE LAYERS:
115 g/4 oz chestnut mushrooms,
thinly sliced
50 g/2 oz butter
225 g/8 oz spinach
115 g/4 oz ricotta cheese
pinch of grated nutmeg

This lovely recipe is suitable for many celebrations and festive occasions. It is delicious served with a creamy mushroom sauce (see page 138), or you could eat it with cranberry and Cumberland sauces at Christmas.

1 Fry the onion and garlic in the butter over low heat, until soft and golden. Transfer with a slotted spoon to a large mixing bowl.

2 Stir in the ground and chopped nuts, breadcrumbs, mashed swede, herbs, cayenne, nut butter, lemon rind and juice. Bind together with

the beaten egg and vegetable stock, and season well with salt and pepper.

3 Fry the chestnut mushrooms in the butter until they are golden brown. Set aside to cool a little.

4 Pick over the spinach leaves, removing any thick stalks, and wash well to remove any dirt. Put in a saucepan, cover with a lid and place over low heat. Cook for a few minutes until the spinach softens and turns bright green. Drain well, pressing out any moisture. Chop the drained spinach and mix with the ricotta cheese, nutmeg and seasoning.

5 Butter a 1-kg/2-lb loaf tin generously and spoon in one-third of the nut mixture. Press down well and cover with the chestnut mushrooms. Cover with half of the remaining mixture, and spread with the spinach

Fritto Misto

and ricotta. Top with the remaining nut mixture and level the top.

6 Bake in a preheated oven at 190°C, 375°F, Gas Mark 5 for 45-50 minutes, until cooked and golden brown on top. Serve sliced with a creamy mushroom sauce (see page 138).

Serves 6-8

Garbanzo **Burritos**

These tortilla parcels are stuffed with a spicy filling of garbanzos (chick peas), but you could use frijoles (refried beans, see page 50) instead. Like other Mexican dishes, they taste particularly good if served with a tomato salsa, guacamole (see page 141) and soured cream.

8 fresh flour tortillas
salsa (see page 16) or tomato
sauce (see page 32)
75 g/3 oz grated Cheddar cheese
guacamole and soured cream, to serve

FOR THE GARBANZO FILLING:
1 tablespoon vegetable oil
2 onions, chopped
1 garlic clove, crushed

1 red pepper, seeded and chopped
1 small dried hot red chilli, crumbled
225 g/8 oz ripe tomatoes,
skinned and chopped
1 tablespoon tomato purée
1 x 400-g/14-oz can
chick peas, drained
salt and freshly ground black pepper
4 spring onions, finely chopped
175 g/6 oz grated Cheddar cheese

1 Make the garbanzo filling. Heat the oil and fry the onions until soft and golden. Add the garlic and red pepper and fry for 3-4 minutes, until softened. Stir in the chilli, tomatoes, tomato purée and drained chick peas. Simmer for 8-10 minutes. Season to taste with salt and pepper.

2 Spread out the tortillas and place some of the garbanzo filling on each one. Sprinkle with the spring onions and Cheddar cheese. Fold up each tortilla around the filling like a

parcel, folding in the sides to seal it. Secure the burritos with wooden cocktail sticks and place them in a large buttered ovenproof dish.

3 Cover the dish with a sheet of foil and bake in a preheated oven at 180°C, 350°F, Gas Mark 4 for 15 minutes. Remove the foil, spoon a little salsa or fresh tomato sauce over the top, sprinkle with grated Cheddar cheese and pop under a hot grill, until the cheese is golden

brown and bubbling. Serve with guacamole and soured cream.

Serves 4

Other fillings

1 Grated Cheddar cheese, chopped hot green chillies and refried beans.

2 Chopped grilled peppers and aubergine, cream cheese and fresh coriander.

Cheese and Potato Fritters

1 tablespoon olive oil
2 leeks, washed, trimmed
and chopped
1 onion, finely chopped
75 g/3 oz mushrooms, chopped
450 g/1 lb mashed
potato, cooled
115 g/4 oz Cheddar or Gruyère
cheese, grated
3 tablespoons chopped fresh herbs,
e.g. parsley, chives, oregano, basil
salt and freshly ground
black pepper
3 tablespoons flour

good pinch of cayenne pepper
olive oil for frying

FOR THE RED ONION
MARMALADE:
15 g/¹/2 oz butter
1 tablespoon olive oil
450 g/1 lb red onions,
very thinly sliced
200 ml/7 fl oz red wine
3 tablespoons wine vinegar
1 teaspoon sugar
salt and freshly ground
black pepper

This is a great way of using up cold mashed potato and odds and ends of cheese. If you are calorie-conscious and don't want to fry the fritters, you can bake them for 15-20 minutes in a preheated oven at 190°C, 375°F, Gas Mark 5. Serve them with red onion marmalade and a rocket and radicchio salad.

1 Make the red onion marmalade: heat the butter and oil and sweat the red onions over very low heat for

about 10 minutes until softened and almost caramelized. Add the wine, wine vinegar and sugar and simmer gently for 30-40 minutes, until thick, reduced and jammy. Season to taste.

2 Heat the olive oil in a frying pan and fry the leeks and onion until soft and golden. Stir in the mushrooms and fry for another 2-3 minutes. Drain off any surplus oil.

3 In a mixing bowl, mix the fried vegetables with the mashed potato, grated cheese and herbs. Season to taste with salt and pepper, and then shape into 8 rounds.

4 Mix the flour and cayenne pepper, and use to dust the potato cakes. Heat some olive oil in a large frying pan and fry the potato cakes over moderate heat until crisp and golden

Garbanzo Burritos

brown on both sides, turning them halfway through cooking.

5 Remove and drain the hot fritters on kitchen paper and serve immediately with the red onion marmalade and a crisp salad.

Serves 4

Snacks & Fast Foods

Vegetable stir-fries, quiches, tarts, pizzas and toasts make healthy snacks and fast food.

Have fun experimenting with all the different toppings, fillings and variations to create

new dishes which will become firm family favourites.

Thai Stir-fried **Vegetables**

3 tablespoons groundnut oil

1 onion, sliced

3 garlic cloves, finely chopped

1 large fresh red or green chilli,
seeded and sliced

1 x 5-cm/2-in piece fresh root ginger,
peeled and chopped

1 red pepper, seeded and sliced

1 green pepper, seeded and sliced

small bunch spring onions,
trimmed and sliced

2-3 kaffir lime leaves, torn

115 g/4 oz mange-tout, trimmed

115 g/4 oz baby sweetcorn

115 g/4 oz mushrooms, quartered,
e.g. chestnut or shiitake

115 g/4 oz shredded spring greens

2 tablespoons soy sauce

2 tablespoons rice wine or
dry sherry

1 teaspoon sugar

25 g/1 oz fresh basil or coriander
leaves, chopped

115 g/4 oz roasted cashew nuts

1 Heat the groundnut oil in a large wok or deep frying pan. Add the onion, garlic, chilli and ginger, and then stir-fry over fierce heat for about 1 minute.

2 Add the peppers, spring onions and kaffir lime leaves, and stir-fry for 2-3 minutes. Then stir in the mange-tout, baby sweetcorn, mushrooms and spring greens. Continue stir-frying for 2 minutes. The vegetables should be heated through but should still be slightly crisp.

3 Add the soy sauce, rice wine or sherry and the sugar. Stir for 1-2 minutes to coat all the vegetables, then throw in the basil or coriander and the cashew nuts. Serve immediately while the vegetables are still sizzling with fried noodles or some plain boiled rice.

Serves 4

Opposite: Stir-fried Vegetables

You can make this dish as hot as you like by adding more chillies. Of course, you don't have to follow the recipe slavishly – the whole point of stir-fries is that you can add virtually any vegetables, herbs or spices and still create a marvellous meal in minutes. In fact, the most time-consuming part of this dish is cutting and preparing all the vegetables.

Greek **Spinach** Pie

You can eat this pie, layered with spinach, feta cheese and filo pastry, either hot or cold. Good fruity olive oil, unsalted butter and salty feta cheese are essential for authenticity.

3 tablespoons extra-virgin olive oil
1 onion, thinly sliced
1 bunch spring onions, trimmed and thinly sliced
1 kg/2 lb fresh spinach, washed, stalks removed and shredded
4 tablespoons chopped flat-leaf parsley
2 tablespoons chopped dill
4 medium eggs
225 g/8 oz feta cheese, crumbled
3 tablespoons double cream
salt and freshly ground black pepper
pinch of grated nutmeg
50 g/2 oz unsalted butter, melted
450 g/1 lb filo pastry

1 Heat the olive oil and then fry the onion until soft and golden. Add the spring onions and then fry for 2-3 minutes. Stir in the spinach until it is glistening with olive oil. Cover the pan and cook over gentle heat for 5 minutes. Stir in the parsley and dill, then remove the vegetables with a slotted spoon and drain well on kitchen paper.

2 Beat the eggs in a clean bowl and then stir in the feta cheese, cream, seasoning and nutmeg. Mix with the drained, cooked vegetables.

3 Brush a 25-cm/10-in square baking tin with plenty of melted butter. Unfold the filo pastry and use a sheet to line the tin, trimming it to fit. Brush with melted butter, then lay another sheet on top. Build up another 4 or 5 layers in this way, buttering between each one.

4 Cover with the cheese and spinach mixture and level the top. Cover with another 4 or 5 sheets of filo pastry, buttering between the sheets. Brush the top layer generously with the remaining melted butter, and mark it into serving portions with the point of a sharp knife, cutting just through the top 2 layers of filo.

5 Bake in a preheated oven at 180°C, 350°F, Gas Mark 4 for about 40 minutes, until puffed up, crisp and golden brown. Serve hot or cold with a crisp green salad.

Serves 6

Vegetable Tatin

This is a savoury variation on the classic sweet tarte tatin, which is made with apples.

1 green pepper
1 yellow pepper
25 g/1 oz butter
1 tablespoon sugar
1 tablespoon white wine vinegar
900 g/2 lb red onions, peeled
1 tablespoon chopped rosemary and thyme
salt and freshly ground black pepper
225 g/8 oz puff pastry

1 Grill the peppers until the skin is blistered and charred. Skin them, removing the stems and seeds. Cut into large chunks.

2 Melt the butter in a large, shallow, cast-iron flameproof dish over moderate heat. Stir in the sugar and wine vinegar. Cut the onions in half and arrange them, on their sides, in the buttery mixture in the base of the pan, packing them in quite tightly.

3 Tuck the peppers between the onions and sprinkle with the chopped herbs, salt and pepper. Cook for 5 minutes. Cover and cook in a preheated oven at 180°C, 350°F, Gas Mark 4 for 30-40 minutes. Remove, and increase the oven temperature to 200°C, 400°F, Gas Mark 6.

4 Roll out the pastry and cut out a round or oval, depending on the shape of the dish – it should be a little larger than the dish. Place the pastry on top of the onions and tuck in the edges round the inside of the dish.

5 Return to the hot oven and bake for 25-30 minutes, until the puff pastry is well risen, crisp and golden. Cool before inverting the dish and turning out the tatin.

Serves 4-6

Mushroom and Goat's Cheese Tart

Tarts and quiches make versatile vegetarian food because there are so many different fillings you can use. If you don't like goat's· cheese, you can use Gruyère or Cheddar instead in this recipe.

225 g/8 oz plain flour
pinch of salt
115 g/4 oz butter, diced
1 egg yolk
cold water, to mix

FOR THE FILLING
25 g/1 oz butter
1 onion, chopped
225 g/8 oz mushrooms, thinly sliced
115 g/4 oz firm goat's cheese
2 large eggs
1 egg yolk
300 ml/¹/₂ pint double cream
pinch of grated nutmeg
2 tablespoons chopped parsley and chives
salt and freshly ground black pepper

Variations

You can fill the pastry case with one of the following alternative fillings and then pour the egg and cream mixture over the top and bake in the same way.

1 Onions (1 kg/2 lb) cooked slowly over low heat until caramelized.

2 Cooked fresh spinach and cream cheese.

3 Young asparagus boiled until tender with grated Gruyère cheese.

4 Sautéed sliced leeks and peppers with sun-dried tomatoes and herbs.

5 Sautéed sliced courgettes, rosemary and grated Cheddar cheese.

6 Crumbled blue cheese and thinly sliced spring onions.

7 Thinly sliced tomatoes, chopped fresh herbs and grated Swiss, mozzarella or Cheddar cheese.

8 Fresh peas, baby asparagus tips, canned artichoke hearts, chopped tarragon and chervil.

9 Parboiled broccoli florets, grated nutmeg and Swiss cheese.

10 Sautéed sliced onions, roasted red pepper strips, black olives and grated cheese.

1 Make the pastry: sift the flour and salt into a mixing bowl and rub in the butter until the mixture resembles fine breadcrumbs. Stir in the egg yolk and enough cold water to mix to a smooth, well-blended ball of dough, which leaves the sides of the bowl clean.

2 Wrap the dough in some foil or greaseproof paper and rest in the refrigerator for at least 15 minutes.

3 Roll out the dough on a lightly floured surface and use to line a buttered 25-cm/10-in fluted loose-bottomed tart tin. Chill in the refrigerator for at least 15 minutes, then line with greaseproof paper or crumpled foil and fill with baking beans. Bake 'blind' in a preheated oven at 180°C, 350°F, Gas Mark 4 for 15-20 minutes. Remove the paper or foil and beans. Leave to cool.

4 Make the mushroom and goat's cheese filling: heat the butter in a frying pan and then fry the onion gently over low heat until softened and golden. Add the mushrooms and continue cooking for 10-15 minutes, until they are softened and turning golden brown. Drain off any of the pan juices.

5 Spoon the onion and mushrooms evenly over the base of the baked

pastry case and scatter with the crumbled goat's cheese.

6 Whisk the eggs, egg yolk and cream together. Season with nutmeg and stir in the parsley and chives. Add a little salt and pepper, and pour over the mushroom filling.

7 Place the tart on a baking sheet and bake in a preheated oven at 180°C, 350°F, Gas Mark 4 for 30-40 minutes, until the filling is just set and still ever so slightly wobbly. Serve the tart warm or cold, cut into wedges.

Serves 6

Loaded **Potato** Skins

You can top scooped-out jacket potatoes with a variety of different toppings. Serve as a snack or as a main meal with salad. Don't throw away the potato flesh. Mash it up and use to make bubble and squeak or Cheese and Potato Fritters (see page 76).

8 medium-sized baking potatoes
25 g/1 oz butter
salt and freshly ground
black pepper
225 g/8 oz grated Cheddar or
Swiss cheese

TO SERVE:
shredded lettuce, salsa (see page 16) and guacamole (see page 141)

1 Scrub the potatoes and bake in a preheated oven at 200°C, 400°F, Gas Mark 6 for about 1 hour, until tender.

2 Cut each potato in half lengthways and scoop out most of the flesh, leaving a little potato around the inside of each skin. Spread a little butter inside the potatoes and season with salt and pepper.

3 Fill the hollow in each potato half with grated cheese and place the potatoes, cheese-side up, in a foil-lined grill tray. Pop under a preheated hot grill for 5 minutes, until the filling is golden brown and bubbling.

4 Serve the potato skins with some shredded lettuce, hot salsa and guacamole.

Serves 4

Variations

You can fill the scooped-out potatoes with any of the following:

1 Chopped tomatoes and spring onions, then sprinkle with cheese and grill.

2 Soured cream, chopped spring onions and snipped chives.

3 Fromage frais mixed with chopped fresh coriander and diced avocado.

4 Frijoles (see page 50), then top with cheese and grill.

5 Soft goat's cheese mixed with grilled peppers and herbs.

6 Home-made coleslaw.

7 Creamy fromage frais blended with green or red pesto sauce.

Nachos with Guacamole

These Tex-Mex snacks are now popular all over the United States. Serve them with pre-dinner drinks or as party food.

1 Heat the oil and gently fry the onion and garlic until soft and golden. Add the tomatoes, chillies, cumin and sugar, and simmer until the sauce reduces and thickens. Season to taste with salt and pepper.

2 Arrange the tortilla chips on a large, shallow ovenproof dish, and spoon the chilli sauce over the top, putting a little on each one. Sprinkle the Cheddar cheese over them and bake in a preheated oven at 180°C, 350°F,

2 tablespoons vegetable oil
1 onion, chopped
2 garlic cloves, crushed
4 large tomatoes, skinned and chopped
2 fresh green chillies, seeded and chopped
pinch of ground cumin
pinch of sugar
salt and freshly ground black pepper

225 g/8 oz tortilla chips
115 g/4 oz grated Cheddar cheese
150 ml/¼ pint soured cream
115 ml/4 fl oz guacamole (see page 141)
diced onion and tomato, to garnish
1 fresh green chilli, seeded and cut into slivers

Gas Mark 4 for 5-10 minutes, until the cheese melts and starts to bubble.

3 Serve the nachos piping hot with bowls of soured cream and guacamole, garnished with diced onion and tomato, and slivers of hot green chilli.

Serves 4-6

Opposite: Nachos with Guacamole

Mediterranean Vegetable Tart

Serves 6

This colourful tart is full of the bold flavours of the Mediterranean: luscious tomatoes, vibrant peppers, fresh young courgettes and velvety aubergines. Serve the tart with a lightly dressed green salad and some crusty bread for a perfect lunch.

225 g/8 oz shortcrust pastry (see page 141)
50 g/2 oz grated vegetarian Parmesan or Cheddar cheese
1 tablespoon olive oil
few sprigs of basil and oregano

FOR THE FILLING:
1 medium aubergine, cubed
2 courgettes, cubed
3 tablespoons olive oil
1 small onion, finely chopped
1 small red pepper, seeded and diced
1 small yellow pepper, seeded and diced
2 garlic cloves, crushed
450 g/1 lb ripe tomatoes, skinned and chopped
1 tablespoon tomato purée
pinch of sugar
salt and freshly ground black pepper.

Cook over low heat for 5-10 minutes, until the tomato sauce has reduced and thickened slightly. Season to taste with salt and pepper.

4 Fill the pastry case with the cooked vegetable mixture. Sprinkle the grated Parmesan or Cheddar cheese over the top, and then drizzle with the olive oil. Bake in a preheated oven at 200°C, 400°F, Gas Mark 6 for about 20 minutes. If the tart looks as though it is browning too much, cover it with some foil and then reduce the oven temperature to 180°C, 350°F, Gas Mark 4. Serve the tart warm, garnished with little sprigs of basil and oregano.

1 Roll out the pastry on a lightly floured surface and use to line a greased 25-cm/10-in deep flan tin. Prick the base with a fork and line with foil and baking beans. Bake 'blind' in a preheated oven at 200°C, 400°F, Gas Mark 6 for 15 minutes. Remove the foil and beans and set aside to cool.

2 Meanwhile, make the filling. Put the aubergine and courgettes in a colander and sprinkle with salt.

Leave for 20 minutes to exude their bitter juices. Rinse them well under running cold water and then pat dry with kitchen paper.

3 Heat the oil and sauté the onion gently until soft and transparent, without colouring. Add the peppers and garlic and cook gently for 2-3 minutes, stirring occasionally. Add the aubergine and courgettes, and cook gently for 5 minutes. Stir in the tomatoes, tomato purée and sugar.

Pizza

If you're in a hurry, you can use a ready-made pizza base but it doesn't taste as good as the real thing. Making the dough does not take very long, but you have to allow time for it to rise. Alternatively, you can rustle up a quick pizza with a vacuum-packed pizza base, a pitta bread, a toasted muffin or some sliced ciabatta brushed with olive oil and then toasted. Cover with one of the suggested toppings and then bake in a preheated oven or pop under a hot grill, and you can eat really delicious, healthy fast food.

25 g/1 oz fresh yeast
300 ml/¹/₂ pint warm water
450 g/1 lb strong plain flour
1 teaspoon salt
2 tablespoons olive oil

FOR THE TOPPING:
4 tablespoons olive oil
1 garlic clove, crushed
1 x 400-g/14-oz can chopped tomatoes
1 tablespoon tomato purée
1 tablespoon chopped oregano
salt and freshly ground
black pepper
6 pieces sun-dried tomatoes
in oil, sliced
115 g/4 oz sliced onion or
mushrooms (optional)
75 g/3 oz black olives, pitted
225 g/8 oz mozzarella cheese,
thinly sliced

1 Blend the yeast with a little of the warm water in a small bowl. Sift the flour and salt into a large mixing bowl, make a well in the centre and pour in the blended yeast, oil and warm water. Gradually draw in the flour and mix to a soft dough.

2 Turn out the dough on to a lightly floured surface and knead well until it is smooth, pliable and elastic. Place the ball of dough in a bowl, cover with a cloth and leave in a warm place for 1 hour, until well risen and doubled in bulk.

3 Turn out the dough on to a lightly floured surface, punch it down and divide into 4 pieces. Knead each piece lightly and roll out until it is about 30 cm/12 in in diameter. Place each pizza on an oiled metal baking sheet and brush with a little olive oil.

4 While the dough is rising, make the tomato sauce for the topping. Heat 2 tablespoons of the olive oil and toss the garlic in it. Add the tomatoes and simmer for 15 minutes, or until the sauce is thick and reduced. Stir in the tomato purée, oregano and seasoning.

Pizza toppings

Here are some ideas for delicious toppings.

1 Over the tomato sauce, scatter thinly sliced onion rings, capers, sultanas, pine nuts and olives. Top with sliced mozzarella cheese.

2 Brush the base with olive oil and scatter with sliced cherry tomatoes, basil, olives and crumbled goat's cheese.

3 Over the tomato sauce, arrange oiled chunks of aubergine and courgette and thinly sliced red onions. Sprinkle with chopped oregano and mozzarella.

4 Brush the base with green or red pesto sauce and top with char-grilled peppers and grated vegetarian pizza cheese.

5 Arrange some sautéed leeks over the tomato sauce and sprinkle with diced fontina and crumbled ricotta cheeses.

5 Spread the tomato sauce over the pizzas and scatter the sun-dried tomatoes, sliced onion or mushrooms (if using) and olives over the top. Finally, scatter the mozzarella cheese over the topping and drizzle with the remaining olive oil.

6 Bake in a preheated oven at 220°C, 425°F, Gas Mark 7 for 12-15 minutes, until the base of the pizza is crisp and golden brown.

Serves 4

Opposite: Pizza

Bruschetta with Garlic

The ultimate quick snack – grilled garlic-flavoured, crusty country bread with a delicious savoury topping.

8 slices crusty country-style bread
2 garlic cloves, peeled and halved
4 tablespoons fruity olive oil
sea salt

1 Grill the slices of bread on both sides, then rub one side of each slice with the cut garlic cloves.

2 Drizzle the olive oil over the top, sprinkle with sea salt and enjoy, or top with one of the suggested toppings savoury (right).

Serves 4

Toppings for bruschetta

1 Grilled sliced red and yellow peppers with ground black pepper.

2 Chopped ripe tomatoes and basil or oregano.

3 Sliced tomato, black olives and grilled goat's cheese.

4 Scrambled eggs and chives.

5 Caramelized onions to which balsamic vinegar has been added.

6 Red onion marmalade (see page 76).

7 Pesto sauce and mozzarella.

8 Olive tapenade or sun-dried tomato paste, radicchio and grilled Taleggio.

9 Creamed mushrooms (see page 24).

10 Walnuts, watercress and creamy Gorgonzola or Stilton.

11 Aubergine slices brushed with olive oil, then grilled.

12 Cottage cheese or ricotta with lots of chopped herbs.

Crostini Toasts

These are often confused with bruschetta, but they are much smaller. Use a thinly sliced French bread flute to make these wonderful 'little toasts'. They are ideal for parties, or for serving with drinks before dinner. Like bruschetta, you can top them with a wide range of different toppings.

1 small French flute
4-5 tablespoons olive oil
sea salt

1 Slice the bread thinly and toast one side under a preheated hot grill.

2 Brush the untoasted side of each slice of bread with olive oil and pop back under the grill until crisp and golden.

3 Sprinkle with a little sea salt and top with any one of the suggested bruschetta toppings (above) or one of the savoury ideas (right).

Serves 4-6

Toppings for crostini

1 Hummus sprinkled with paprika, lemon juice and olive oil.

2 Sliced pear, rocket and creamy goat's cheese.

3 Tsatsiki, grilled aubergine and chopped fresh mint.

4 Pan-fried sliced apple and blue cheese.

5 Fried tofu, chilli sauce, fresh coriander and grilled cheese.

6 Sun-dried tomato paste with feta cheese.

Mozzarella in Carrozza

This is the perfect snack food for eating 'on the hoof' as thousands of people in Rome and other Italian cities do on their way to work each morning. Use only the real Italian mozzarella packed in water.

8 slices of white bread
225 g/8 oz mozzarella, drained and sliced
2 large eggs
2 tablespoons milk
olive oil for frying

1 Cut the crusts off the bread. Divide the mozzarella between 4 slices of the bread and cover with the remaining slices. Press them firmly together.

2 Beat the eggs and milk together in a bowl, and then dip the mozzarella sandwiches briefly into this mixture. They should soak up the egg on both sides.

3 Fry the sandwiches, one at a time, in a frying pan in hot olive oil for 3-4 minutes each side, until crisp and golden. Drain on kitchen paper, and cook the remaining sandwiches in the same way. Cut each sandwich in half and eat immediately.

Serves 4

Stuffed Croissants

Shop-bought croissants can be warmed through and filled with a savoury mixture, or topped with grated cheese and popped under a preheated hot grill. Alternatively, you can fill them with fruit or chocolate for a sweet snack or quick pudding.

4 croissants
1 quantity creamy mushrooms
(see page 24)
25 g/1 oz grated Swiss cheese

1 Place the croissants under a hot grill or in a preheated oven at 180°C, 350°F, Gas Mark 4 for a few minutes, just long enough to warm them through.

2 Then split the croissants in half langthways and fill with the hot creamy mushroom mixture. Sandwich them back together and sprinkle with grated cheese.

Savoury fillings

1 Put some sliced Cheddar or Swiss cheese on both sides of the croissants, pop back under the grill until the cheese melts and sandwich together with sliced tomato or watercress. Alternatively, use plum tomatoes and Mozzarella.

2 Fill with fried sliced onions, and mushrooms topped with Dijon mustard and melted cheese.

3 Fill the croissants with creamy scrambled eggs and sautéed sliced button mushrooms sprinkled with chopped parsley.

4 Spread the split croissants with mayonnaise or natural fromage frais and then fill with shredded crisp cos lettuce, feta cheese and avocado.

Sweet fillings

1 Fill with mascarpone cheese and shavings of really dark chocolate, then flash under a hot grill to melt the chocolate.

2 Fill with puréed apple or quince cooked in

butter and sweetened with brown sugar, and crème fraîche.

3 Fill with fromage frais or ricotta and fresh raspberries dusted with icing sugar.

3 Place the croissants under the hot grill or pop them back in the oven for 2-3 minutes, until the cheese melts.

Serves 4

Beanburgers and Red Pepper Relish

You can make delicious burgers with puréed cooked beans, chick peas and lentils. Serve straight out of the pan with red pepper relish.

1 Put the beans in a bowl, cover with cold water and leave them to soak overnight. Drain and place in a saucepan with fresh water. Bring to the boil, then simmer for 1-1¼ hours, until tender. Drain well and then set aside to cool.

2 Meanwhile, make the red pepper relish. Gently fry the onion in the olive oil until golden. Add the sugar and balsamic vinegar, turn up the heat and cook quickly until the liquid evaporates and turns syrupy. Grill or roast the peppers and garlic cloves. Skin, seed and chop the peppers. Peel and mash the garlic cloves. Stir the chopped peppers, mashed garlic flesh and coriander into the onion mixture. Season with salt and pepper to taste.

3 Put the cooled beans in a food processor or blender with the onion, garlic, chilli (if using), parsley, egg,

225 g/8 oz dried haricot or
cannellini beans
1 small onion, chopped
2 garlic cloves, crushed
1 fresh red chilli, chopped (optional)
few sprigs of parsley
1 egg
pinch of grated nutmeg
75 g/3 oz grated Gruyère cheese
2 tablespoons fromage frais
squeeze of lemon juice
salt and freshly ground
black pepper
oil for frying

FOR THE COATING:
1 egg, beaten
115 g/4 oz fresh breadcrumbs

FOR THE RED PEPPER RELISH:
1 onion, chopped
2 tablespoons olive oil
pinch of sugar
1 tablespoon balsamic vinegar
2 red peppers
2 garlic cloves
1 tablespoon chopped
fresh coriander
salt and freshly ground black pepper

nutmeg and grated Gruyère cheese. Process until puréed, then add the fromage frais, a squeeze of lemon juice and some salt and pepper.

4 Chill the bean mixture in the refrigerator for at least 30 minutes, then divide it into 8 or 12 portions and, with floured hands, shape each one into a round.

5 Dip each round in beaten egg and then into the breadcrumbs until

evenly coated. Shallow fry in hot oil until crisp and golden on both sides. Drain on kitchen paper. Serve with warm red pepper relish.

Serves 6

Spiced **Onion** Rings

4 large onions, thinly
sliced in rings
150 ml/¼ pint milk
115 g/4 oz sifted plain flour
2 tablespoons cornflour
2 teaspoons hot chilli powder
1 teaspoon paprika
good pinch of salt
good pinch of caster sugar
oil for deep frying

Serve these red-hot fried onion rings with vegetable burgers or beanburgers (above).

1 Put the onion rings in a bowl and pour the milk over the top. Leave to soak for at least 30 minutes. Remove the onions and drain well.

2 Mix the flour, cornflour, chilli powder, paprika, salt and sugar in a

shallow dish. Dip the onions in the seasoned flour, shaking off any excess flour.

3 Quickly deep fry the onions in hot oil at 190°C, 375°F, until they are evenly crisp and golden. Remove with a slotted spoon and drain on kitchen paper. Serve the onion rings immediately.

Serves 4-6

Cajun Grilled **Vegetables**

Grilled blackened vegetables sprinkled with cajun spices can be served simply with soured cream or yogurt flavoured with mint.

4 plum tomatoes, halved
2 aubergines, sliced
2 red onions, quartered
450 g/1 lb pumpkin, peeled and sliced
2 red peppers, seeded and quartered
25 g/1 oz pine nuts
115 ml/4 fl oz olive oil
1 tablespoon ground cajun spices
sea salt and freshly ground
black pepper

FOR THE SALAD GARNISH:
115 g/4 oz peppery salad leaves,
e.g. rocket, watercress

3 tablespoons extra-virgin
olive oil
1 tablespoon balsamic vinegar
115 g/4 oz feta cheese, cubed

FOR THE SAUCE:
150 ml/1/4 pint thick Greek yogurt
or soured cream
squeeze of lemon juice
3 tablespoons finely
chopped fresh mint
freshly ground sea salt and ground
black pepper

1 Prepare all the vegetables and spread them out in a grill pan lined with foil. Scatter the pine nuts over the top and drizzle with olive oil, paying particular attention to the aubergines. Sprinkle the cajun spices evenly over the vegetables.

2 Cook under a preheated grill until the vegetables are tender and charred, but not burnt. Turn the aubergines, tomatoes and pumpkin over when they look golden brown and slightly charred around the edges on one side. Brush occasionally with the spicy olive oil in the grill pan. Season with salt and pepper.

3 Wash and spin the salad leaves. Mix the olive oil and balsamic vinegar, and toss the leaves and feta cheese in this dressing. Arrange on a serving plate with the hot Cajun grilled vegetables.

4 Mix the yogurt or soured cream with the lemon juice, mint and seasoning to taste. Serve chilled with the grilled vegetables and salad.

Serves 4

Roasted Italian-style **mushrooms**

Large open-capped field mushrooms make a delicious snack on toast. If possible, use Fontina cheese in this recipe, as it melts to a wonderful consistency.

8 large 10-cm/4-in diameter
field mushrooms
3 tablespoons olive oil
2 tablespoons chopped parsley
1 tablespoon snipped chives
2 garlic cloves, crushed
salt and freshly ground
black pepper
8 slices crusty round bread
350 g/12 oz Fontina cheese

1 Arrange the mushrooms, stem side up, in a foil-lined grill pan. Mix the olive oil with the chopped herbs and garlic, and brush gently over the mushrooms. Season with salt and freshly ground black pepper.

2 Place under a preheated hot grill for about 4-5 minutes, until the mushrooms are heated through and softened. Remove and cut each mushroom into 1-cm/1/2-in wide strips.

3 Toast the bread lightly on both sides. Slice the Fontina cheese into 1-cm/1/2-in wide strips. Arrange the mushrooms and Fontina alternately on the slices of toasted bread.

4 Place the toasts on a baking sheet and bake in a preheated oven at 200°C, 400°F, Gas Mark 6 for 5 minutes. Serve immediately.

Serves 4

Side dishes & Salads

The following recipes for vegetable side dishes and some sensational salads can be served as an accompaniment to the main meal. They are incredibly varied, including baked gratins, fritters, stir fries and even a barbecued salad.

Provençal **Vegetable** Gratin

You can make a gratin with almost any vegetables. They can be layered, or mixed into a creamy sauce, or moistened with stock or cream, but they must be baked in an oiled or buttered ovenproof dish until tender, and topped with crisp breadcrumbs and grated cheese.

1 Place the aubergine slices in a colander and sprinkle with salt. Set aside for 30 minutes to drain their bitter juices. Rinse well under running cold water and then dry on some kitchen paper.

2 Fry the sliced aubergine, onions and garlic in 5 tablespoons of the olive oil until golden brown. Spread the fried vegetables over the base of a shallow ovenproof dish.

3 With a potato peeler, carefully remove strips of peel lengthways from the sides of the courgettes to leave vertical green stripes and then slice the courgettes thinly.

4 Arrange the courgettes and tomatoes in alternate rows on top of the aubergine mixture, overlapping them like fish scales. Brush lightly with the remaining olive oil, season and scatter with the chopped herbs.

5 Bake in a preheated oven at 190°C, 375°F, Gas Mark 5 for 20 minutes. Sprinkle with breadcrumbs and Parmesan cheese, drizzle with olive oil, and then bake for a further 10 minutes, until crisp and golden.

Serves 4

Opposite: Provençal Vegetable Gratin

---

1 aubergine, sliced
2 onions, thinly sliced
2 garlic cloves, crushed
6 tablespoons olive oil
3 large courgettes
3 large tomatoes, skinned and sliced
salt and freshly ground black pepper
1 tablespoon chopped thyme and rosemary

FOR THE TOPPING:
4 tablespoons fresh white breadcrumbs
2 tablespoons grated vegetarian Parmesan cheese
1 tablespoon olive oil

Other vegetable gratins

1 Thinly sliced potatoes layered with chopped onion and garlic, moistened with vegetable stock or boiling milk and cream, and sprinkled with breadcrumbs and grated Gruyère cheese.

2 Sliced christophene cooked until tender, drenched in a creamy white sauce and scattered with chopped parsley, breadcrumbs, paprika and grated cheese, then popped under a hot grill.

Baked **Fennel** Niçoise

4 large round fennel bulbs
25 g/1 oz butter
1 tablespoon olive oil
25 g/1 oz fresh breadcrumbs
1 tablespoon grated vegetarian
Parmesan cheese
salt and freshly ground
black pepper
1 tablespoon chopped fennel leaves
or flat-leaf parsley

This dish has a delicious aniseed flavour but works well with celery.

1 Cut off the bases and hard stalks of the fennel bulbs, reserving any feathery leaves. Wash thoroughly and then cut each bulb in half from top to bottom.

2 Cook the fennel in salted boiling water for 15-20 minutes, until just tender but not soft. Drain well and leave to cool.

3 Cut the cooled fennel lengthways into thick slices and arrange them, overlapping each other, in a buttered ovenproof dish. Dot them with butter and drizzle the olive oil over the top. Sprinkle with the breadcrumbs and grated Parmesan cheese, then season.

4 Bake in a preheated oven at 200°C, 400°F, Gas Mark 6 for 15 minutes, until golden brown. Sprinkle the fennel or parsley over the top.

Serves 4-6

French **Potato** Bake

This is really easy to assemble and can be made well in advance for cooking later. For a really special variation, add some soaked dried porcini to the potatoes and sprinkle the top with grated cheese.

1 kg/2 lb potatoes
1 onion, finely chopped
1 leek, washed, trimmed and
finely chopped
2 garlic cloves, crushed
salt and freshly ground
black pepper
300 ml/½ pint hot vegetable stock
(or stock and milk)
40 g/1½ oz butter, diced
1 tablespoon finely
chopped parsley

1 Peel the potatoes and slice them thinly lengthways. Cover the base of a well-buttered ovenproof dish with a layer of potato slices.

2 Sprinkle some of the chopped onion and leek over the potatoes, then scatter a little garlic and seasoning over the top. Continue layering up in this way until all the vegetables are used up, finishing with a layer of potatoes.

3 Pour the hot vegetable stock

slowly over the potatoes, so that it all sinks in. If wished, you can now cover the potato bake with some foil and set aside in a cool place until needed.

4 When ready to cook, dot the top with butter, and bake in a preheated oven at 180°C, 350°F, Gas Mark 4 for 30-40 minutes, until the top is crisp and golden. Sprinkle the potato bake with chopped parsley before serving.

Serves 4

Other vegetable bakes

1 Drained, cooked cauliflower or broccoli coated in a blue cheese sauce, sprinkled with breadcrumbs and grated Parmesan and grilled until browned.

2 Sliced boiled beetroot layered with grated cheese, covered in cream and topped with breadcrumbs and cheese. Dot with butter and bake for 10-15 minutes.

3 Sliced or puréed cooked pumpkin, layered with grated Gruyère cheese, sprinkled with breadcrumbs and grated cheese, then dotted with butter and baked for 5-10 minutes.

Rosemary-scented **Courgettes**

This is a lovely aromatic summer dish. Plain boiled, steamed or fried courgettes can be dull, but the addition of fresh rosemary and some cream transforms them into something special.

1 kg/2 lb courgettes
2 tablespoons fruity green
olive oil
15 g/¹/₂ oz butter
few sprigs of fresh rosemary
150 ml/5 floz crème fraîche
salt and freshly ground black pepper

1 Trim the ends off the courgettes and slice them thickly. Cook them in lightly salted boiling water for 3-4 minutes, then drain well.

2 Heat the olive oil and butter in a saucepan, and add the drained courgettes and sprigs of rosemary. Cover the pan and cook very gently over low heat for about 5 minutes, until the courgettes are just starting to turn golden.

3 Stir in the crème fraîche carefully without damaging the courgettes, and cook gently for about 5 minutes, until the sauce reduces and the courgettes are tender. Season to taste with salt and lots of freshly ground black pepper. Serve immediately.

Serves 4-6

Louisiana **Sweetcorn** Fritters

These little crunchy fritters from the Deep South of the United States go well with most vegetable and bean chilli dishes, or they can be served as a savoury snack at parties.

50 g/2 oz plain flour
pinch of salt
1 egg, beaten
4-5 tablespoons milk
150 g/5 oz drained canned
sweetcorn or cooked
corn kernels
1 small green pepper, seeded
and finely chopped
1 small fresh red chilli, seeded
and finely chopped
pinch of paprika
groundnut oil or unsalted
butter for frying

TO SERVE:
salsa, guacamole, soured cream,
chopped red onion, lime wedges

1 Sift the flour and salt into a bowl and beat in the egg. Add enough milk, beating well, to make a really smooth batter with a thick, creamy consistency. Leave to stand for at least 30 minutes.

2 Stir the sweetcorn kernels, green pepper, chilli and paprika into the batter, then drop a few spoonfuls of the mixture into some hot groundnut oil or butter. Fry gently until golden brown underneath and then turn the fritters over and cook the other side.

3 Remove the hot cooked fritters, drain on kitchen paper and keep warm. Cook the remaining fritters in the same way until all the batter is used up.

4 Serve the fritters very hot with salsa, guacamole or chopped avocado, soured cream, chopped red onion and wedges of lime.

Serves 6

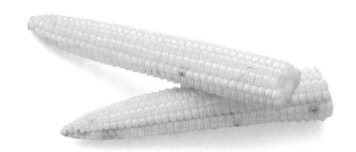

Roasted Winter **Vegetables**

2 medium carrots, peeled
and halved
4 small parsnips
1 small swede, peeled and
cut into wedges
2 potatoes, peeled and
cut into wedges
450 g/1 lb pumpkin, peeled
and sliced thickly
2 fat leeks, washed, trimmed
and quartered
2 sweet potatoes, peeled and sliced
1 small celeriac, peeled and
cut into large chunks
few sprigs of thyme or rosemary
sea salt and ground black pepper
1 garlic clove, crushed
4-5 tablespoons olive oil

Most winter root vegetables lend themselves well to roasting. Serve them with quiches, grilled tofu, nut roast or beanburgers, or on their own with fromage frais and chilli sauce. You don't have to follow the recipe – just use the seasonal vegetables of your choice.

1 Prepare all the vegetables and spread them out in a large roasting pan or shallow ovenproof dish. Tuck the herbs down between the vegetables and sprinkle with salt and pepper and the crushed garlic. Drizzle the olive oil over the top and turn the vegetables gently in the oil.

2 Roast in a preheated oven at 200°C, 400°F, Gas Mark 6 for 30-40 minutes, until the vegetables are cooked and tender.

Serves 4-6

Roasted summer vegetables

Roasted vegetables taste equally good in summer, especially served outside with salads and barbecued food. Roast them in exactly the same way; choose from the following: asparagus, aubergines, corn cobs, courgettes, mushrooms, onions, peppers, shallots and tomatoes. Sprinkle with oregano, marjoram, rosemary and olive oil before roasting.

Roman **Cauliflower**

1 large cauliflower
4 tablespoons extra-virgin
olive oil
2 fresh red chillies, seeded
and finely chopped
(or 2 dried chillies)
salt and freshly ground
black pepper

This hot, spicy way of cooking cauliflower is popular in Rome. You can cook romanesco cauliflowers, broccoli, winter greens and purple sprouting broccoli in the same way.

1 Cut off the thick stalk and outer leaves from the cauliflower. Cut in half, remove the core and divide the cauliflower into florets.

2 Cook the florets in lightly salted boiling water until just tender but still very firm. Drain well and then dry on kitchen paper.

3 Heat the olive oil in a large heavy frying pan. Add the chillies and fry very gently over low heat for about 5 minutes to flavour the oil.

4 Add the drained cauliflower florets and stir gently in the hot oil until evenly covered. Turn up the heat a little and cook for a few minutes until heated through. Sprinkle some freshly ground black pepper over the cauliflower florets and serve immediately.

Serves 4

Opposite: Roasted Winter Vegetables

Hungarian **Lecso**

3 tablespoons olive oil
1 large onion, thinly sliced
4 green peppers, seeded and sliced
4 large ripe tomatoes, skinned and chopped
2 teaspoons sugar
1 tablespoon paprika
salt and freshly ground black pepper
1 tablespoon chopped flat-leaf parsley

TO SERVE:
soured cream and caraway seeds

In Hungary, plain boiled or steamed vegetables are unknown. The Hungarians love rich, colourful vegetable stews, flavoured with spices or fresh seasonal fruit. Lecso is characteristic of their fiery, distinctive style of cooking. Be sure to use really ripe red tomatoes and good-quality paprika in this dish.

1 Heat the olive oil and fry the onion gently over low heat until softened and golden. Stir in the green peppers and simmer for 10-15 minutes, until the peppers are soft.

2 Stir in the tomatoes, sugar and paprika, and continue cooking for about 15 minutes, until the mixture thickens and reduces. Season to taste with salt and pepper, and add another pinch of sugar if necessary.

3 Serve hot sprinkled with flat-leaf parsley, with a dollop of soured cream and some caraway seeds.

Serves 4

Green **Beans** with Chilli

If you get fed up with boiled green beans, try this delicious Chinese stir-fried dish. Serve it with rice or noodles.

450 g/1 lb thin green beans
3 tablespoons vegetable or sesame oil
2 garlic cloves, crushed
1 x 2.5-cm/1-in piece fresh root ginger, peeled and chopped
1 fresh red chilli, seeded and finely chopped
4 spring onions, trimmed and sliced
good pinch of salt
50 g/2 oz cashew nuts
115 ml/4 fl oz vegetable stock
2 tablespoons light soy sauce
1 tablespoon sherry
1 teaspoon sugar
freshly ground black pepper

1 Top and tail the beans and remove the 'strings' along their sides. Heat the oil in a wok or deep frying pan, and add the garlic, ginger and chilli. Stir-fry for 1 minute over moderate heat. Stir in the spring onions and salt, and fry for 1 minute.

2 Add the green beans and cashew nuts, and stir-fry for 1 minute. Add the vegetable stock, soy sauce, sherry and sugar, and turn up the heat. When the liquid starts to boil, reduce the heat and let it bubble away for 4-5 minutes, stirring occasionally, until the liquid reduces and the beans are tender. Sprinkle with plenty of black pepper and serve.

Serves 4

Indian Spiced **Potatoes**

675 g/1½ lb potatoes, peeled
4-5 tablespoons vegetable oil
1 fresh chilli, finely chopped
2 garlic cloves, crushed
½ teaspoon cumin seeds
½ teaspoon mustard seeds
1 teaspoon ground turmeric
½ teaspoon salt
¼ teaspoon chilli powder

TO SERVE:
115 ml/4 fl oz natural yogurt
1 tablespoon chopped
fresh coriander
mango chutney

Serve these golden spiced potatoes with chilled yogurt sprinkled with chopped fresh coriander leaves, and some mango chutney.

1 Cook the potatoes in boiling salted water until they are just tender but still firm. Drain well, then set aside to cool. When cool, cut them into dice.

2 Heat the oil in a large frying pan and add the chilli, garlic, cumin and mustard seeds. Fry for 2-3 minutes, without browning the garlic, until the spices release their aroma.

3 Stir in the turmeric, salt and chilli powder, and then add the diced

potatoes. Fry gently over moderate heat until the potatoes are crisp, golden brown, heated through, and coated with spices.

4 Serve the spiced potatoes very hot with yogurt, sprinkled with coriander, and mango chutney.

Serves 4-6

Green Beans with Chilli

Rosti Potato Cakes

Rosti is a traditional Swiss way of cooking potatoes. Here, instead of preparing a large dish of rosti, the grated potato is mixed with celeriac and made into little crisp fritters.

450 g/1 lb potatoes
565 g/1¼ lb celeriac
3 eggs, beaten
1 onion, grated
1 garlic clove, crushed
1 tablespoon flour
2 tablespoons chopped parsley and chives
pinch of grated nutmeg
salt and freshly ground black pepper
vegetable oil for frying

1 Peel the potatoes and cut away the outer skin from the celeriac. Grate them coarsely with a grater or in a food processor. Put them in a sieve and rinse under running cold water. Drain well and then pat dry with kitchen paper.

2 Put the potatoes and celeriac in a large bowl with the eggs, and mix well together. Stir in the onion, garlic, flour, herbs and nutmeg. Season with salt and pepper.

3 Divide the potato mixture into 12-16 equal-sized portions, and then shape them into small rounds with your hands.

4 Heat the oil in a frying pan and fry the potato cakes, a few at a time, until crisp and golden brown on both sides – turn them halfway through cooking. Drain on kitchen paper, and serve very hot.

Serves 4-6

Stir-fried Mushrooms

You can use large dark field mushrooms or a mixture of different mushrooms in this traditional Chinese stir-fry. Try little brown chestnut mushrooms or oriental shiitake and oyster mushrooms.

4 tablespoons vegetable or groundnut oil
4 spring onions, finely chopped
2 garlic cloves, crushed
225 g/8 oz spring greens, washed and shredded
450 g/1 lb mushrooms, quartered or sliced
1 teaspoon chilli bean sauce or chilli powder (optional)
2 tablespoons dark soy sauce
1 tablespoon rice wine or dry sherry
pinch of sugar
salt and freshly ground black pepper
1 tablespoon chopped fresh coriander leaves

1 Heat the oil in a wok or a deep frying pan. When it is hot, throw in the spring onions and garlic and stir-fry for 2 minutes.

2 Stir in the spring greens and cook briskly, turning them in the oil until they turn bright green. Add the mushrooms and continue stir-frying for 2-3 minutes.

3 Add the chilli bean sauce or chilli powder (if using) together with the soy sauce, rice wine or sherry and a pinch of sugar. Continue stir-frying for a few more minutes until the liquid evaporates and the mushrooms are tender. Check the seasoning before adding salt and pepper. Sprinkle with chopped coriander and serve immediately.

Serves 4

Caramelized **Onions**

Use small pickling onions in this dish and keep a close eye on them while they are cooking to ensure that they do not burn. Serve with Cheese and Potato Fritters or Beanburgers.

450 g/1 lb pickling onions
1 tablespoon sugar
15 g/½ oz butter
salt and freshly ground
black pepper

1 Peel the onions and arrange in a single layer in a large frying pan. Sprinkle with sugar, dot with butter and barely cover with cold water.

2 Cover the pan and bring to the boil, then uncover and cook vigorously until the liquid evaporates and the onions are coated in a golden brown syrup. Watch them closely when the sugar starts to caramelize

Roasted onions

This is a good way of serving larger onions. Peel the onions and put them in a roasting pan. Brush them generously with olive oil and melted butter, and bake in a preheated oven at 180°C, 350°F, Gas Mark 4 for about 45 minutes. Serve sprinkled with a dusting of sea salt.

and shake the pan to turn the onions in the syrup. Season with salt and pepper and serve immediately.

Serves 4

Leeks in Parsley Sauce

This is a wonderful way of serving leeks, or broad beans, carrots or broccoli for that matter. The sauce should be light and creamy, barely coating rather than drowning the leeks.

900 g/2 lb leeks, washed, trimmed
and roughly chopped

FOR THE SAUCE:
300 ml/½ pint milk
1 onion stuck with 2 cloves
bouquet garni
salt and freshly ground
black pepper
25 g/1 oz butter
25 g/1 oz flour
small bunch parsley,
finely chopped
150 ml/¼ pint double cream
squeeze of lemon juice

1 Make the sauce. Put the milk, onion and bouquet garni in a saucepan with a little salt and pepper and bring to the boil. Reduce the heat to the barest simmer, and heat through very gently for 30 minutes. Strain, reserving the flavoured milk.

2 Melt the butter in a pan and stir in the flour. Cook for 2 minutes, without browning, then gradually

beat in the flavoured milk, until you have a smooth, thick sauce. Cook very gently over low heat for 10-15 minutes. Season to taste and stir in the parsley and cream.

3 Meanwhile, cook the leeks in lightly salted boiling water for 3-4 minutes, until they are just tender. Drain well. Stir the leeks into the hot parsley sauce, then add a squeeze of lemon juice and transfer to a serving dish.

Serves 4

Fruity Red Cabbage

Red cabbage can be cooked with many winter fruits, including apples, pears, juniper berries and cranberries. Unlike most other vegetables, it can be cooked in advance and actually tastes even better when it has been reheated.

2 tablespoons groundnut or vegetable oil
1 onion, finely chopped
8 juniper berries, crushed
2 cooking apples, peeled, cored and diced
115 g/4 oz cranberries
565 g/1¼ lb red cabbage, shredded
pinch of ground cinnamon
pinch of ground allspice
pinch of grated nutmeg
1 tablespoon brown sugar
115 ml/4 fl oz red wine
1 tablespoon red wine vinegar
salt and freshly ground black pepper
1 tablespoon redcurrant jelly (optional)

1 Heat the oil in a large flameproof casserole, and gently fry the onion until soft and golden. Add the crushed juniper berries, diced apples, and cranberries, and cook gently for 2-3 minutes.

2 Stir in the red cabbage, spices, sugar, wine and wine vinegar. Stir well, then cover the casserole dish and place in a preheated oven at 180°C, 350°F, Gas Mark 4 for about 1 hour, or until the cabbage is tender. Season to taste and, if wished, stir in the redcurrant jelly.

Serves 4-6

Barbecued Salad

225 g/8 oz thin asparagus stalks, trimmed
1 red pepper, seeded and cut into thick strips
1 yellow pepper, seeded and cut into thick strips
8 spring onions, trimmed
1 radicchio, trimmed and cut into wedges
oil for brushing
small bunch of rocket
225 g/8 oz baby spinach leaves
salt and freshly ground black pepper

FOR THE DRESSING:
4 tablespoons fruity green olive oil
1 tablespoon balsamic vinegar
squeeze of lime juice
pinch of sugar
1 tablespoon chopped basil
1 tablespoon chopped fresh coriander leaves

This may sound bizarre but it is a brilliant colourful salad with a distinctive smoky flavour. The vegetables and salad leaves are seared quickly on a grill over hot coals, tossed in a herb vinaigrette and eaten warm. It is characteristic of the new healthy and thoughtful style of Californian cooking.

1 Cook the asparagus in salted boiling water for 4-5 minutes. Drain well. Brush the peppers and spring onions with olive oil and place on a grill over hot coals. Grill quickly, turning frequently and brushing with more oil if necessary, until the vegetables are just starting to char.

2 Brush the radicchio with oil and grill for 1-2 minutes each side, with the asparagus. Toss the rocket and baby spinach leaves on the grill – just long enough to wilt them.

3 Mix all the dressing ingredients together and toss the barbecued vegetables lightly in the herb dressing. Season with salt and pepper, and serve warm.

Serves 4

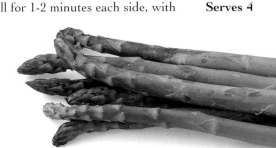

Leeks Niçoise

675 g/1½ lb slim leeks
2 hard-boiled eggs, peeled
and chopped
1 tablespoon chopped parsley
75 g/3 oz black olives, pitted

FOR THE DRESSING:
115 ml/4 fl oz extra-virgin
olive oil
2 tablespoons white
wine vinegar
2 teaspoons Dijon mustard
½ teaspoon sugar
salt and freshly ground
black pepper

This warm leek salad is popular throughout France, but in Provence it is served with black olives and hard-boiled eggs. Use slim leeks rather than fat ones. You can serve thin green beans or asparagus in the same way.

1 Trim the leeks, removing the dark green leaves. Wash them thoroughly under running cold water to remove any dirt.

2 Cook the leeks in salted boiling water for 8-10 minutes, until just cooked and tender. Drain well and dry on kitchen paper.

3 While the leeks are cooking, make the dressing. Mix the olive oil and wine vinegar, then stir in the Dijon mustard and sugar until smooth. Season with salt and pepper.

4 Arrange the warm leeks in a serving dish and pour the dressing over the top. Sprinkle the chopped egg over the leeks and scatter with parsley. Serve the leeks warm with some black olives.

Serves 4-6

Leeks Niçoise

Christmas Salad

A fresh-tasting salad makes a welcome change at Christmas after all the rich food. This salad uses seasonal winter leaves and fresh fruit and cheese.

2 heads chicory
1 radicchio
1 red onion, finely chopped
2 red apples, cored and cubed
115 g/4 oz roughly chopped
walnuts
115 g/4 oz Stilton cheese,
cubed
1 avocado, peeled, stoned and thinly
sliced
3 tablespoons chopped parsley
and chives

FOR THE DRESSING:
4 tablespoons olive oil
1 tablespoon red wine vinegar
freshly ground black pepper

1 Wash and trim the chicory and radicchio, and separate them into leaves. Arrange in a salad bowl with the red onion, apples, walnuts, Stilton and avocado.

2 Mix the dressing ingredients together and then toss the salad gently until everything is glistening with oil. Sprinkle the chopped parsley and chives over the top and serve immediately.

Serves 4-6

Greek Bean Salad

Cannellini or borlotti beans can be substituted for black-eyed beans in this classic Greek salad of cos lettuce and feta cheese.

225 g/8 oz dried black-eyed beans
1 red onion, thinly sliced
4 ripe tomatoes, quartered
leaves of 1 cos lettuce
75 g/3 oz black olives, pitted
175 g/6 oz feta cheese, cubed
1 tablespoon snipped chives
1 tablespoon chopped fresh coriander

FOR THE DRESSING:
4 tablespoons fruity green Greek
olive oil
juice of 1/2 lemon
1 garlic clove, crushed (optional)
pinch of sugar
salt and freshly ground
black pepper

1 Soak the black-eyed beans beans in some cold water overnight. Drain, rinse under running cold water and put the beans in a saucepan. Cover with fresh water and bring to the boil.

Reduce the heat and cook gently for about 1 hour until the beans are tender but not mushy. Drain well.

2 Mix the beans with the red onion, tomatoes and cos lettuce in a large salad bowl. Mix the dressing ingredients together and gently toss the bean salad.

3 Scatter the olives, feta cheese, snipped chives and chopped coriander over the salad, and serve.

Serves 4-6

Caesar Salad with Grilled **Goat's Cheese**

leaves of 1 cos lettuce
175 g/6 oz round chèvre (goat's cheese), cut into 4 slices

FOR THE DRESSING:
2 eggs
115 ml/4 fl oz fruity olive oil
juice of 1 lemon
dash of Worcestershire sauce
50 g/2 oz freshly grated vegetarian Parmesan cheese
salt and freshly ground black pepper

FOR THE GARLIC CROÛTONS:
4 thick slices crusty white bread
2 tablespoons olive oil
2 garlic cloves, crushed

This salad tastes fantastic with garlic croûtons and grilled goat's cheese. You could also top it with slices of grilled tofu.

1 Make the garlic croûtons: remove the crusts from the bread and cut into dice. Put the olive oil and garlic in a bowl and toss the bread in it. Put the croûtons on a baking sheet and cook in a preheated oven at 180°C, 350°F, Gas Mark 4 for 5-10 minutes, until crisp and golden. Set aside to cool.

2 Make the dressing: boil the eggs in their shells for 1 minute and then run some cold water over them. Break the eggs into a bowl and beat well. Whisk in the olive oil slowly in a thin, steady stream. Stir in the lemon juice, Worcestershire sauce, Parmesan cheese and seasoning.

3 Put the cos lettuce in a large salad bowl and toss in the dressing. Add the garlic croûtons and toss again. Divide the Caesar Salad between 4 serving plates.

4 Quickly grill the slices of goat's cheese until softened and just starting to ooze and turn brown. Arrange them on top of the salad and serve immediately.

Serves 4

Celeriac Salads

More good winter salads for when you are getting fed up with the usual seasonal hot root vegetables. You have the choice of a vinaigrette dressing or a mustardy mayonnaise.

1 Trim and peel the celeriac and cut into julienne (matchstick) strips, dropping them into a bowl of cold water and lemon juice.

2 Bring a saucepan of water to the boil and tip in the celeriac. Bring back to the boil and cook for 1 minute, then drain and rinse under running cold water. Pat dry with kitchen paper or a clean cloth.

3 Now prepare one of the salads. For the vinaigrette, mix the celeriac with

1 large celeriac
juice of 1 lemon

FOR THE VINAIGRETTE SALAD:
2-3 Cox's apples, cored and diced
50 g/2 oz chopped walnuts
3 tablespoons olive or walnut oil
1 tablespoon white wine vinegar
salt and freshly ground black pepper

1 tablespoon finely chopped parsley

FOR THE MUSTARDY SALAD:
150 ml/¼ pint mayonnaise
150 ml/¼ pint fromage frais
2 teaspoons whole-grain or Dijon mustard
squeeze of lemon juice
salt and freshly ground black pepper
1 tablespoon finely chopped parsley

the apples and walnuts in a bowl. Blend the oil, wine vinegar and seasoning and pour over the celeriac mixture. Toss gently together, sprinkle with parsley and serve.

4 For the mustardy salad, mix together the mayonnaise (home-made

if possible) with the fromage frais, mustard and lemon juice. Season to taste, then stir in the blanched strips of celeriac. Sprinkle with parsley and serve.

Serves 4

Warm **Potato** Vinaigrette

At any time of year, this warm potato salad is a welcome addition to a meal. Use red-skinned or waxy new potatoes if possible. Many supermakets now sell special salad new potato varieties.

675 g/1½ lb new potatoes, washed but not peeled
1 bunch spring onions, chopped
3 tablespoons chopped fresh chives

FOR THE DRESSING:
4 tablespoons extra-virgin olive oil
1 tablespoon white wine vinegar
salt and freshly ground black pepper

1 Cook the new potatoes in lightly salted boiling water until tender but not mushy. Drain well and cut in half or into smaller pieces.

2 Mix the potatoes with the spring onions. Mix the dressing and pour over the potatoes and onions. Toss lightly, sprinkle with chives and serve while still warm.

Serves 4

Variations

1 Instead of chives, add a mixture of chopped summer herbs, e.g. mint, oregano and tarragon.

2 Mix the warm potatoes with chopped fresh red chilli, chopped red onion and fresh coriander, then toss in the vinaigrette.

3 Substitute crème fraîche or soured cream for the vinaigrette dressing, and sprinkle with plenty of chopped chives.

Warm Spinach Salad

Warm **Spinach** Salad

You must use young tender baby spinach leaves for this salad, not the older, larger leaves which can be very fibrous with tough stems. It can be served as a first course or even as a light meal if you add cherry tomatoes, sliced avocado, hard-boiled eggs, and mozzarella, feta or goat's cheese. Or, for a touch of real luxury, serve with quail's eggs.

2 red peppers
115 ml/4 fl oz extra-virgin olive oil
350 g/12 oz wild mushrooms, e.g.
cèpes, chanterelles, girolles
3 tablespoons balsamic vinegar
pinch of sugar
salt and freshly ground
black pepper
225 g/8 oz baby spinach leaves
75 g/3 oz chopped walnuts
1 tablespoon chopped parsley

1 Put the red peppers under a preheated hot grill, and grill, turning occasionally, until the skins are blistered and charred. Place the peppers in a polythene bag until cool, then peel off the skins, remove the seeds and cut into thin strips.

2 Heat 4 tablespoons of the olive oil in a small frying pan, and add the mushrooms. Fry gently for about 5 minutes, until cooked. Add 2 tablespoons of the balsamic vinegar and a good pinch of sugar, and continue cooking for 1 minute. Season to taste with salt and pepper and set aside while you quickly prepare the spinach salad.

3 Wash and dry the spinach leaves and put them in a bowl with the walnuts. Mix the remaining olive oil and balsamic vinegar and use to toss the spinach.

4 Divide the dressed spinach and walnuts between 4 plates and arrange the warm wild mushrooms and their pan juices, and the grilled red pepper strips on top. Sprinkle with chopped parsley and serve.

Serves 4

Crunchy **Carrot** Salad

This is a good winter salad, which is especially good at Christmas. As an alternative, you can mix the vegetables, fruit and nuts with some mayonnaise and fromage frais, and use it as a topping for baked jacket potatoes.

4 large carrots
2 sticks celery
1 small onion
2 red apples
50 g/2 oz raisins
75 g/3 oz chopped hazelnuts
or almonds
2 tablespoons sesame seeds

1 tablespoon snipped chives
2 tablespoons chopped parsley

FOR THE DRESSING:
5 tablespoons olive oil
juice of 1/2 lemon
pinch of sugar
salt and freshly ground black pepper

1 Peel the carrots and cut them into matchstick-sized sticks. Trim the celery and cut into dice. Peel and grate the onion. Cut the apples in half, scoop out the cores and cut the flesh into dice.

2 Put the carrots, celery, onion and apples in a large bowl with the raisins, chopped nuts and sesame seeds, and mix well.

3 Mix all the dressing ingredients together and pour over the carrot mixture. Toss gently so everything is coated with the dressing, then chill in the refrigerator for at least 30 minutes.

4 Serve the carrot salad, sprinkled with chopped chives and parsley.

Serves 4

Mexican Baja **Salad**

This is typical of the new breed of salads eaten on the Baja peninsula and on the West Coast of the United States. Serve it with tacos, burritos and other Mexican or Tex-Mex dishes.

75 g/3 oz cos or crisp green lettuce
75 g/3 oz curly endive (frisée)
75 g/3 oz rocket
1 small radicchio
1 large carrot
1 courgette, diced or thinly sliced
1 red pepper, seeded and chopped
1 red onion, finely chopped
6-8 cherry tomatoes, halved
small bunch of chives, snipped

few coriander leaves, roughly chopped

FOR THE DRESSING:
1 avocado, peeled and stoned
4 tablespoons olive oil
1 tablespoon wine vinegar
squeeze of lime juice
1 fat garlic clove, crushed
freshly ground black pepper

1 Wash the salad leaves thoroughly and spin dry. Separate the radicchio into leaves, then wash well and dry. Place all the salad leaves in a large salad bowl.

2 Peel the carrot and then, using the same potato peeler, peel off long strips. Add to the salad leaves with the courgette, red pepper, red onion and cherry tomatoes.

3 Make the dressing. Mash the avocado flesh with a fork, and then beat in the olive oil, wine vinegar, lime juice and garlic until well blended. If the dressing is too thick, add a little more olive oil. Season with plenty of freshly ground black pepper.

4 Toss the salad gently in the dressing and sprinkle with snipped chives and chopped coriander. Serve immediately before the dressing starts to discolour.

Serves 4-6

Spanish **Roasted Vegetable** Salad

This Catalan speciality is better known in Spain as *escalivada*. The vegetables can be roasted in the oven or, if you prefer a smoky, slightly charred flavour, cooked on a grill over hot coals. You can eat this salad either warm or cold.

1 large aubergine
1 red pepper
1 green pepper
2 Spanish onions
2 courgettes
6 fat garlic cloves, unpeeled
sprigs of fresh thyme and rosemary
6 tablespoons olive oil
sea salt and freshly ground black pepper
4 ripe tomatoes
2 tablespoons sherry vinegar
juice of 1/2 lemon
2 tablespoons chopped parsley

1 Place the aubergine, red and green peppers, onions and courgettes in a large roasting pan. Tuck the garlic cloves and sprigs of fresh thyme and rosemary into the gaps between the vegetables.

2 Drizzle the olive oil over all the vegetables and season with salt and pepper. Bake in a preheated oven at 180°C, 350°F, Gas Mark 4 for 30-40 minutes, adding the tomatoes after 15 minutes.

3 Let the vegetables cool a little, then slice the aubergine and courgettes thickly, and seed and slice the peppers. Cut the onions into wedges, and halve or quarter the tomatoes. Arrange all the vegetables on a large serving platter.

4 Peel the roasted garlic cloves and mash the flesh into the olive oil pan juices. Mix in the sherry vinegar and lemon juice, and pour over the roasted vegetables. Sprinkle with chopped parsley and serve with crusty bread to mop up the delicious garlic dressing on the plates.

Serves 4-6

Greek Country **Salad**

The addition of salty feta cheese turns a fresh rustic salad into a light lunch for summer. Serve with hard-boiled eggs and some crusty bread. You could grill some peppers and aubergines until slightly charred, and then slice them over the salad.

1 cos lettuce
1/2 cucumber, sliced thinly
4 large ripe tomatoes, skinned
and quartered
bunch of spring onions, trimmed
and sliced
6 sprigs of fresh mint, chopped
1 tablespoon chopped
fresh oregano
2 tablespoons chopped parsley
or coriander leaves
225 g/8 oz feta cheese, cubed
75 g/3 oz black olives
lemon quarters, to serve

FOR THE DRESSING:
5 tablespoons fruity green
olive oil
juice of 1 lemon
pinch of sugar
salt and freshly ground black pepper

1 Wash the cos lettuce, trim the base and separate the leaves. Dry them thoroughly, then shred the leaves and place them in a large salad bowl.

2 Add the cucumber, tomatoes, spring onions and chopped herbs to the lettuce in the bowl, and toss together lightly.

3 Blend the olive oil and lemon juice for the dressing with the sugar, and season with salt and pepper. Pour over the salad and toss gently.

4 Scatter the feta cheese over the salad and serve with black olives and lemon quarters.

Serves 4

Goat's Cheese and Puy Lentil Salad

If you can't get the tiny greenish-black Puy lentils for this warm winter salad, you can use brown lentils instead.

225 g/8 oz Puy lentils
1 bay leaf
8 cherry tomatoes, halved
50 g/2 oz watercress or rocket
175 g/6 oz goat's cheese, cubed
1 tablespoon chopped parsley
1 tablespoon snipped chives

FOR THE DRESSING:
6 tablespoons extra-virgin olive oil
2 tablespoons lemon juice
1/2 teaspoon Dijon mustard
salt and freshly ground
black pepper

1 Put the lentils in a sieve and wash them under running cold water. Drain and tip the lentils into a saucepan. Add the bay leaf and cover with plenty of cold water. Bring to the boil and continue boiling for 15-20 minutes, until the lentils are cooked and tender. Drain them in a colander.

2 Mix the warm lentils with the cherry tomatoes, watercress or rocket and goat's cheese in a large salad bowl.

3 Make the dressing: blend the olive oil, lemon juice and mustard, and season with salt and pepper to taste. Toss the lentil salad in the dressing, sprinkle with chopped parsley and chives, and serve immediately while the salad is still warm.

Serves 4

Winter **Venetian** Salad

2 red peppers
2 red radicchios
1 bunch corn salad
1 bunch rocket leaves
small bunch watercress
mozzarella cheese, to serve
freshly ground black pepper

FOR THE DRESSING:
4 tablespoons extra-virgin olive oil
1 tablespoon balsamic vinegar
juice of 1/2 lemon

Colourful salads of radicchio and crisp bitter leaves are popular in Venice, where they are eaten in a simple dressing of olive oil, vinegar and lemon juice.

1 Put the red peppers under a preheated hot grill, turning them occasionally, until the skins are blistered and charred all over. Remove the peppers and place in a polythene bag. When cool, remove the skins and seeds, and cut the peppers into strips.

2 Blend the olive oil with the balsamic vinegar and lemon juice. Put all the salad leaves in a bowl and toss in the dressing. Scatter the grilled red pepper strips over the top. Serve with mozzarella cheese dressed with a little olive oil and sprinkled with freshly ground black pepper.

Serves 4

Satay Salad

This Thai salad combines warm vegetables in a spicy dressing flavoured with coconut milk, curry paste and peanuts. You can buy a hot curry paste if you don't want to make it yourself.

3 carrots, peeled and cut into matchstick strips
115 g/4 oz shredded cabbage
115 g/4 oz thin green beans, trimmed
1 red pepper, seeded and sliced
1 green pepper, seeded and sliced
115 g/4 oz bean sprouts
115 g/4 oz canned water chestnuts, drained and sliced
2 tablespoons chopped fresh coriander leaves

FOR THE DRESSING:
2 tablespoons groundnut oil
1 tablespoon curry paste
300 ml/1/2 pint coconut milk
2 tablespoons soy sauce
2 teaspoons brown sugar
1 teaspoon ground coriander
2 teaspoons ground cumin
juice of 1 lime
3 tablespoons crushed roasted peanuts or peanut butter
salt and freshly ground black pepper

1 Blanch the carrots, cabbage, green beans and peppers in boiling water for 3-4 minutes, until just tender but still crisp. Drain well and mix with the bean sprouts and water chestnuts in a large salad bowl.

2 Heat the groundnut oil and stir in the curry paste. Cook gently for 1 minute, then add the coconut milk, soy sauce, brown sugar, spices and lime juice. Stir in the peanuts and simmer gently for 3-4 minutes. Season.

3 Remove from the heat, allow to cool a little and then pour the warm dressing over the vegetables and toss well. Serve warm, sprinkled with coriander.

Serves 4

Hot curry paste

2.5-cm/1-in piece fresh root ginger, peeled and chopped
4 fresh red chillies, seeded and chopped
1 stalk lemon grass, chopped
1 small onion, finely chopped
2 garlic cloves, crushed
1 teaspoon coriander seeds
1/2 teaspoon ground cumin
juice of 1/2 lime
3 tablespoons chopped coriander leaves
salt and ground black pepper

Put all the ingredients in a food processor or blender, and process to a paste. Store in a screw-top jar in the refrigerator for up to one week. Use in Thai vegetable curries and stir-fries.

Moroccan **Orange** Salad

4 large oranges
115 g/4 oz baby spinach leaves,
rocket or watercress
115 g/4 oz small black olives
grated rind and juice of 1 orange
3 tablespoons olive oil
dash of white wine vinegar
salt and freshly ground
black pepper
chopped fresh coriander leaves,
to garnish

Oranges are often made into a salad with salt and olives in North Africa and southern Italy. Serve it on a bed of young spinach leaves or some bitter, pungent rocket and watercress.

1 Peel the oranges with a sharp knife, removing all the white pith, then cut the flesh horizontally into thin slices.

2 Arrange the orange slices on top of the spinach, rocket or watercress, and scatter with the black olives.

3 Mix the grated orange rind and juice with the olive oil and a dash of wine vinegar. Pour over the orange salad and season to taste with salt and pepper. Sprinkle with chopped coriander and serve at once.

Serves 4

Lentil and Tomato Salad

Lentils tossed in vinaigrette make an earthy, filling summer salad. Serve it as a main course with hard-boiled eggs and crusty buttered wholemeal bread.

225 g/8 oz brown Continental lentils
1 red onion, finely chopped
4 spring onions, finely chopped
4 ripe tomatoes, quartered
5 tablespoons fruity green
olive oil

1 tablespoon red wine vinegar
pinch of sugar
salt and freshly ground
black pepper
2 tablespoons chopped parsley
and mint

1 Put the lentils in a bowl, cover with cold water and leave to soak for 1 hour. Remove any gritty pieces that float to the surface, then drain the lentils in a sieve.

2 Place them in a saucepan, cover with fresh water and cook for about

1¼ hours, or until tender. Drain the lentils well and then mix in a large bowl with the red onion, spring onions and tomatoes.

3 Blend the olive oil, wine vinegar and sugar together, and pour over

the lentils, onions and tomatoes. Toss gently and season with salt and plenty of black pepper. Sprinkle with the chopped parsley and mint, and serve.

Serves 4

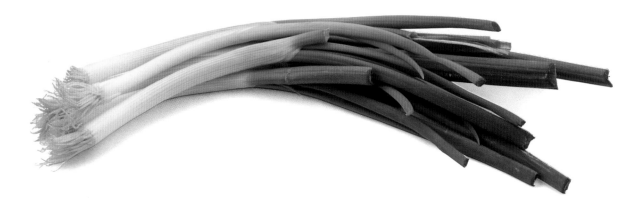

Desserts & Puddings

Here's a selection of hot, comforting puddings, fruity, cold desserts and ice creams and sorbets. What they all have in common is seasonal fruits – soft fruits and berries in summer; apples, pears and dried fruits in winter.

Tropical **Fruit** Kebabs

4 small bananas
1 large mango
1 ripe papaya
1/2 fresh pineapple
4 peaches
50 g/2 oz caster sugar
3 tablespoons dark rum
icing sugar, for dusting

FOR THE CHOCOLATE SAUCE:
150 g/5 oz bitter chocolate
115 ml/4 fl oz double cream

FOR THE FRUIT MASCARPONE:
115 g/4 oz ripe strawberries
1 tablespoon caster sugar
115 g/4 oz mascarpone cheese

Serve these kebabs with a decadently rich hot sauce of melted bitter chocolate. Alternatively, mash some strawberries or raspberries into a bowl of mascarpone cheese and put a spoonful on each dessert plate.

1 Peel the bananas and cut into quarters. Peel and stone the mango and cut the flesh into large chunks. Peel the papaya, remove the seeds and cut into chunks. Remove the peel from the pineapple and slice thickly. Discard the central core, and cut each slice into large chunks. Stone and quarter the peaches.

2 Thread the fruit alternately on to wooden skewers. Sprinkle generously with caster sugar and then place under a preheated hot grill for about 5 minutes. Turn the fruit kebabs frequently so that they caramelize evenly.

3 Meanwhile, make the chocolate sauce: break the chocolate into a basin and set over a saucepan of simmering water until melted. Bring the cream to the boil, and stir into the melted chocolate.

4 Mash the strawberries, sweeten with sugar and then stir into the mascarpone cheese.

5 Heat the rum, set it alight and pour it flaming over the fruit kebabs. Serve immediately, dusted with icing sugar, with the chocolate sauce and strawberry mascarpone.

Serves 4

Other fruit kebabs

1 Thread peeled and quartered apples on to skewers, brush with lemon juice and then with melted butter and sugar. Grill until caramelized and serve with crème fraîche.

2 Thread quartered bananas on to skewers, brush with lemon juice, sprinkle with sugar and grill. Make a toffee sauce by heating 115 g/4 oz butter and 115 g/4 oz brown sugar with a good pinch each of cinnamon and nutmeg. Whisk in 150 ml/1/4 pint double cream.

Tropical Fruit Kebabs

Quick Fruit **Brulée**

565 g/1¼ lb mixed fruits
300 ml/½ pint double cream
175 g/6 oz caster sugar

Make this pudding at any time of the year, adding a variety of seasonal fruits: soft fruits (raspberries, strawberries and redcurrants), peaches, apricots or plums in the summer; bananas, grapes, poached apples or pears in the winter.

1 Prepare the fruits, removing any stones, stalks etc., and, if large, cut into smaller pieces. Tip all the fruits into a large serving dish or, if wished, arrange them in the bases of 4 individual dishes.

2 Whip the cream until it is thick and stands up in soft peaks. Spoon it over the fruits to completely cover them and level the top. Chill in the refrigerator for at least 15 minutes.

3 Put the sugar in a heavy-based saucepan with 4 tablespoons of cold water. Stir over gentle heat until the sugar dissolves. Turn up the heat and boil hard until the sugar syrup turns golden. Keep an eye on it so that as soon as it caramelizes and turns golden brown you can whip it off the heat before it burns.

4 Carefully pour the caramel over the top of the whipped cream to cover it evenly. You must do this immediately. Leave to cool for a few minutes before serving.

Serves 4

Summer Fruit **Tarts**

It's not time consuming to make delicious little tarts if you cheat and use ready-made puff pastry. Buy it freshly made or frozen. Top the tarts with different fruits of varying colours, such as greengages, apricots, peaches, cherries and soft berry fruits.

350 g/12 oz puff pastry
450 g/1 lb mixed
summer fruits
caster sugar, for sprinkling
3 tablespoons apricot jam
1 tablespoon water
squeeze of lemon juice

1 Roll out the puff pastry on a lightly floured surface and cut into rounds, about 7.5 cm/3 in in diameter.

2 Arrange the summer fruits on top of the rounds of pastry. Use stoned and sliced peaches or nectarines; halved and stoned small apricots, greengages or plums; cherries or any other soft berry fruits. Sprinkle lightly with a little sugar.

3 Bake in a preheated oven at 220°C, 425°F, Gas Mark 7 for about 15 minutes, until the pastry is risen and golden, and the fruit is tender.

4 Heat the apricot jam with the water and lemon juice, and stir well. Brush the tarts lightly with the apricot glaze and serve warm with a bowl of whipped cream.

Serves 4-6

Spanish Orange **Rice**

Cold creamy rice puddings, perfumed with orange, are eaten throughout Spain and Mexico. Serve as a chilled summer dessert in a pool of fresh fruit coulis or with a fruit compôte.

> 350 ml/12 fl oz milk
> freshly pared rind of 1 orange
> 50 g/2 oz caster sugar
> 50 g/2 oz pudding rice, rinsed
> 2 egg yolks
> juice of 1 orange
>
> FOR THE CARAMEL:
> 50 g/2 oz caster sugar
> 3 tablespoons water

1 Put the milk and orange rind in a saucepan with the sugar. Heat gently, stirring until the sugar dissolves. Bring to the boil, then stir in the pudding rice and simmer gently for 25-30 minutes, until thickened and creamy.

2 Discard the strips of orange rind. Beat the egg yolks into the creamy rice mixture and then stir in the orange juice.

3 Put the sugar and water for the caramel in a small saucepan. Stir over low heat until the sugar dissolves, and then bring to the boil. Cook rapidly over high heat until it turns a rich golden brown. Pour the caramel into 6 dariole moulds, tilting each one to coat the base and sides.

4 Fill the moulds with the rice mixture and stand them in a roasting pan. Pour in enough warm water to come halfway up the sides of the moulds. Cook in a preheated oven at 180°C, 350°F, Gas Mark 4 for 20-25 minutes.

5 Remove the moulds from the oven and set aside to cool, then chill in the refrigerator until ready to serve. Turn out the moulds and serve the rice puddings with fresh apricot coulis (sweetened sieved apricots) or a fruit compôte of summer berries.

Serves 4

Poached **Pears** in Beaumes de Venise

This makes a wonderful winter dessert – light and refreshing. Serve hot with crème fraîche, vanilla ice cream or some thick natural yogurt.

> 300 ml/¹/2 pint Beaumes de Venise wine
> 300 ml/¹/2 pint water
> 115 g/4 oz sugar
> thinly pared lemon rind
>
> 1 vanilla pod
> 1 cinnamon stick
> 6 dessert pears, firm but ripe
> crème fraîche, to serve

1 Pour the wine and water into a large saucepan. Add the sugar, lemon rind, vanilla pod and cinnamon stick. Stir gently over low heat until the sugar dissolves.

2 Peel the pears, cut them in half and carefully cut out the cores. Place the pears in the liquid in the saucepan and turn up the heat to simmering point. Cover the pan and simmer gently for 10-15 minutes, until the pears are tender.

3 Remove the pears with a slotted spoon and place them in a serving dish. Return the poaching liquid to the heat and bring to the boil. Boil until it reduces by at least half. Remove the vanilla pod and cinnamon stick, and then pour the syrup over the pears. Cool and then chill before serving with crème fraîche.

Serves 4

Strawberry Hazelnut Meringue

A dessert to die for on a hot, sultry summer's day – juicy ripe strawberries and whipped cream sandwiched in crisp nutty meringue. It tastes equally good with raspberries or redcurrants.

1 Break the egg whites into a large bowl and whisk until stiff. Gradually whisk in the sugar, a spoonful at a time, and, lastly, the vinegar. Gently fold the toasted chopped hazelnuts into the meringue.

4 egg whites
225 g/8 oz caster sugar
1/2 teaspoon vinegar
75 g/3 oz toasted hazelnuts, finely chopped
300 ml/1/2 pint double cream
225 g/8 oz strawberries, hulled
icing sugar, for dusting

2 Line two 17.5-cm (7-in) sandwich tins with parchment baking paper, and divide the meringue between the tins. Bake in a preheated oven at 130°C, 250°F, Gas Mark 1/2 for about 1 1/4 hours, until crisp and firm.

3 Leave in the tins until cold and then turn out the meringues. Whip the cream until stiff and then spread it over the meringues. Scatter the strawberries over the meringue base and dust with icing sugar. Place the other meringue on top and dust with more icing sugar. Chill in the refrigerator before serving.

Serves 6

Winter Fruit Compôte

450 g/1 lb mixed no-soak dried fruit, e.g. apricots, figs, peaches, prunes
50 g/2 oz raisins
juice of 2 oranges
1 cinnamon stick
300 ml/1/2 pint water
300 ml/1/2 pint crusted port
25 g/1 oz pistachio nuts

A compôte of dried fruits can be served chilled or warm with cream or vanilla ice cream. It makes a particularly welcome change at Christmas after all the rich meals. If you have a sweet tooth, you can sweeten it with a little brown sugar or honey.

1 Put the mixed dried fruit and raisins in a saucepan with the orange juice, cinnamon stick and water. Cover the pan and simmer gently over low heat for 20 minutes.

2 Remove from the heat and add the crusted port and pistachio nuts. Leave to cool, then pour into a large serving bowl and chill in the refrigerator for several hours. Serve chilled or warm with crème fraîche or vanilla ice cream.

Serves 4

Opposite: Winter Fruit Compôte

Pear frangipane tart

Serves 6

This mouth-watering tart is usually made with pears or apples. Make sure that the pears are not under-ripe, or they will not cook to a succulent softness but will remain hard. In summer, you can substitute poached apricots, peaches or cherries.

115 g/4 oz butter
115 g/4 oz caster sugar
2 eggs
115 g/4 oz ground almonds
15 g/¹/₂ oz plain flour
3 large pears, ripe but firm

FOR THE PASTRY:
200 g/7 oz plain flour
pinch of salt

100 g/3¹/₂ oz butter, cut
into dice
1 tablespoon vanilla sugar
1 large egg yolk
cold water, for mixing

FOR THE APRICOT GLAZE:
75 g/3 oz apricot jam
2 tablespoons water
1 teaspoon lemon juice

1 Make the pastry: sift the flour and salt into a bowl and rub in the butter until the mixture resembles fine breadcrumbs. Add the vanilla sugar, and then bind together with the egg yolk and a little cold water, if necessary. Chill in the refrigerator for 30 minutes. Roll out the pastry and use to line a well-buttered 25-cm/10-in loose-bottomed tart tin. Chill in the refrigerator while you make the filling.

2 Cream the butter and sugar together, then beat in the eggs, one at a time. Beat in the ground almonds and flour. Spread over the base of the prepared pastry case.

3 Peel and halve the pears, carefully removing the cores. Slice each half

Variations

1 Summer fruits include poached apricots, cherries, peaches and raspberries.

2 Winter fruits include apples, blackberries, mango and kiwi fruit.

through thinly at a slight angle, keeping it intact, and then arrange the sliced pear halves in a circle, like the spokes of a wheel, on top of the frangipane filling. Bake in a preheated oven at 200°C, 400°F, Gas Mark 6 for 15 minutes. Reduce the oven temperature to 170°C, 325°F, Gas Mark 3 and bake for a further 15 minutes until the frangipane is firm and golden. Cool a little.

4 Make the apricot glaze: heat the apricot jam with the water and lemon juice, and pass through a sieve. When the tart is just warm, remove it from the tin and lightly brush the top of the frangipane and the pears with the apricot glaze. Serve warm with crème fraîche or thick cream.

Strawberry Zabaglione

In Italy, zabaglione is always served hot straight from the pan, but add some strawberries and cream, and it makes a delicious iced dessert.

300 ml/½ pint double cream
4 egg yolks
5 tablespoons caster sugar
8 tablespoons Marsala
225 g/8 oz strawberries, hulled
sprigs of mint, for decoration

1 Whip the double cream until stiff, then cover and chill throughly in the refrigerator.

2 Put the egg yolks and sugar in the top of a double-boiler or in a basin sitting over a small pan of gently simmering water. Beat the egg yolks and sugar until thick.

3 Add the Marsala and beat with a wire whisk or a hand-held electric whisk until the zabaglione is thick, light and hot. Be patient – it will take 10-15 minutes to thicken.

4 Remove the zabaglione from the heat and cool a little, then fold gently into the chilled whipped cream with a metal spoon.

5 Divide the strawberries, reserving a few for decoration, between 6 tall glasses or serving bowls and spoon the creamy zabaglione over the top.

6 Chill in the refrigerator until needed. Alternatively, you can pop them into the freezer for up to 1 hour. Just before serving decorate the zabaglione with the reserved strawberries and some sprigs of fresh mint.

Serves 6

Baked Amaretto Peaches

Use unblemished, ripe peaches for this recipe. Stuffed peaches are popular in Italy, and you can experiment with savoury fillings as well as sweet ones. Gorgonzola, Taleggio and walnuts all complement the luscious sweetness of the peaches. If wished, you can use nectarines instead of peaches.

4 large peaches
8 amaretti biscuits
1 egg yolk
1 tablespoon caster sugar
50 g/2 oz mascarpone cheese
15 g/½ oz butter
4 tablespoons Amaretto liqueur

FOR THE AMARETTO CHEESE:
3 tablespoons fromage frais
3 tablespoons mascarpone cheese
1 tablespoon sugar
1 tablespoon Amaretto liqueur

1 Wash the peaches and pat dry with kitchen paper. Cut them in half and remove the stones. Carefully hollow out a little of the flesh to enlarge the cavity. Reserve the flesh you have removed for the filling.

2 Crush the amaretti biscuits with a rolling pin and mix well with the egg yolk, caster sugar, mascarpone cheese and reserved peach flesh.

3 Divide the mixture between the peaches and smooth the tops. Stand the stuffed peaches in a buttered baking dish. Dot them with butter, and sprinkle the Amaretto over the top.

4 Bake in a preheated oven at 160°C, 325°F, Gas Mark 3 for about 20 minutes, until golden on top. Alternatively, you can place the peaches under a preheated hot grill for about 5 minutes.

5 Meanwhile, make the Amaretto cheese. Beat the fromage frais into the mascarpone, and stir in the sugar and Amaretto liqueur. Serve with the warm peaches.

Serves 4

Opposite: Strawberry Zabaglione

Strawberry Almond **Shortcakes**

Eat these American shortcakes as a summer dessert or serve with home-made lemonade for afternoon tea. As a change from strawberries, try filling them with raspberries, redcurrants or peaches instead.

300 g/10 oz plain flour
pinch of salt
3 teaspoons baking powder
150 g/5 oz butter, softened
50 g/2 oz caster sugar
150 ml/¼ pint whipping cream
melted butter, for brushing
icing sugar, for dusting

FOR THE FILLING:
75 g/3 oz mascarpone cheese
75 ml/3 fl oz low-fat fromage frais
1-2 tablespoons icing sugar
450 g/1 lb strawberries, hulled
50 g/2 oz toasted flaked almonds

1 Sift the flour, salt and baking powder into a large mixing bowl. Rub in the butter until the mixture resembles breadcrumbs. Stir in the caster sugar and the cream. You should end up with a soft but not too sticky dough.

2 Turn out the dough on to a lightly floured surface and knead gently. Roll it out quite thickly – about 1.25 cm/½ in thick. Cut into 5-cm/2-in rounds with a plain cutter.

3 Arrange half of the shortcakes on a buttered baking sheet and brush lightly with melted butter. Put the remaining shortcakes on top of the buttered ones.

4 Bake in a preheated oven at 230°C, 450°F, Gas Mark 8 for 10-15 minutes, until the shortcakes are well risen and golden brown. Cool a little on a wire rack.

5 While the shortcakes are cooking, mix the mascarpone cheese and fromage frais in a bowl. Sweeten to taste with icing sugar.

6 Split the cooked shortcakes in half while warm. Fill with the strawberries, toasted flaked almonds and mascarpone filling, and sandwich together. Dust lightly with icing sugar and serve.

Serves 6

Peach and Blueberry **Crumble**

This is real comfort food – juicy fruit topped with a buttery, nutty crumble. The wonderful thing about crumbles is that they are so quick and easy to make. You can use almost any fruit; the usual choices are apples, blackberries or rhubarb. However, this version combines tart blueberries with succulent peaches.

1 Cut the peaches into quarters and place in a well-buttered baking dish with the blueberries and sugar. Toss them gently together.

2 Make the crumble: put the flour

6 large peaches, skinned and stoned
225 g/8 oz blueberries
75 g/3 oz sugar

FOR THE CRUMBLE:
175 g/6 oz plain flour
50 g/2 oz ground almonds
175 g/6 oz butter, diced
75 g/3 oz sugar
50 g/2 oz flaked almonds or chopped hazelnuts

and ground almonds in a bowl and rub in the butter with your fingertips until the mixture resembles fine breadcrumbs.

3 Mix in the sugar and almonds or hazelnuts. Sprinkle with a tablespoon of water and stir well.

4 Spread the crumble over the fruit in the baking dish, levelling the top. Sprinkle a tablespoon of water over the top before baking. Bake in a preheated oven at 200°C, 400°F, Gas Mark 6 for 20 minutes, then reduce the oven temperature to 180°C, 350°F, Gas Mark 4 for a further 15 minutes.

4 Serve the crumble hot or warm with some vanilla ice cream, hot custard, whipped cream or crème fraîche, according to choice.

Serves 6

Creole **Grilled Bananas** Flambé

Bananas are eaten throughout the Caribbean in both sweet and savoury dishes. One of the easiest ways of cooking them is to grill them and serve with this wickedly rich toffee sauce.

	FOR THE CREAMY TOFFEE SAUCE:
4 ripe bananas, peeled	300 ml/½ pint double cream
2 tablespoons brown sugar	50 g/2 oz demerara sugar
juice of 1 lime	2 teaspoons black treacle
4 tablespoons dark rum	

1 Put the bananas on a foil-lined grill pan and sprinkle the brown sugar and lime juice over them. Put under a preheated hot grill for a few minutes, turning them until they are golden.

2 Meanwhile, heat the cream, sugar and black treacle in a small pan, stirring to mix. Bring to the boil, and then remove from the heat.

3 Heat the rum and set it alight. Pour the flaming rum over the bananas and serve with the toffee sauce.

Serves 4

Filo Fruit **Parcels**

It is very important when making these little fruit pastries never to let the filo pastry dry out. Cover the paper-thin sheets you are going to use with some greaseproof paper and a damp tea-towel until you are ready for them. Virtually any fruit can be used: the soft berry fruits of summer, autumnal apples, quinces and pears mixed with blackberries from the hedgerow, or the gooseberries and elderflowers of late spring.

175 g/6 oz redcurrants
1 tablespoon cassis (optional)
50 g/2 oz sugar
2 sheets filo pastry
25 g/1 oz butter, melted
115 g/4 oz soft goat's cheese
crème fraîche or thick cream, to serve

FOR THE FRUIT COULIS:
225 g/8 oz mixed raspberries, strawberries and redcurrants
50 g/2 oz caster sugar

1 Make the fruit coulis: put all the fruits and sugar in a large bowl and mix well. Set aside for at least 30 minutes. Tip them into a blender or food processor and process until puréed. Push through a sieve to remove any pips.

2 Carefully pick the redcurrants over, removing any stalks, and soak in the cassis (if using) for 30 minutes. Mix in the sugar.

3 Cut one of the sheets of filo pastry in half lengthways, then cut each piece of pastry into 3 squares, so that you have 6 in total.

4 Brush one filo square with melted butter and lay another square on top, brushing generously with some more melted butter. Then put a spoonful of the goat's cheese in the centre and top with some of the redcurrants.

5 Gather up the edges of the pastry and pull them together in the middle, twisting gently. Repeat with the remaining squares, and then do the same with the other sheet of filo pastry to make 3 more parcels.

6 Put the filo parcels on a buttered baking sheet and bake in a preheated oven at 230°C, 450°F, Gas Mark 8 for 8-10 minutes, until crisp and golden.

7 Serve the filo fruit parcels in a pool of fruit coulis with some crème fraîche or thick cream.

Serves 6

Provençal **Lavender** Ice Cream

300 ml/¹/₂ pint single cream

2 sprigs of lavender

4 egg yolks

150 g/5 oz vanilla sugar

300 ml/¹/₂ pint double cream, whipped

TO SERVE:

50 g/2 oz coarsely chopped toasted almonds

few sprigs of lavender

This delicately flavoured ice cream evokes memories of the lavender-scented hills of Provence. Make it in the summer when your lavender bushes are in bloom. You can make vanilla sugar by storing a vanilla pod in a jar of caster sugar.

1 Put the single cream and sprigs of lavender in a saucepan and heat through gently. Bring it just up to the boil, remove from the heat and leave to infuse for 5 minutes.

2 Beat the egg yolks and vanilla sugar together in a bowl, until thick and creamy. Remove the lavender from the warm cream and beat the cream into the egg mixture.

3 Set the bowl over a small saucepan of simmering water and then stir constantly with a wooden spoon until the custard thickens and coats the back of the spoon. Remove from the heat and set aside to cool.

4 Fold the whipped cream gently into the cooled custard and pour into a deep metal freezing container. Freeze on the lowest possible setting.

5 When the ice cream is partially frozen (the sides are frozen but the middle is still soft), remove from the freezer and stir well or beat with a hand whisk. Return to the freezer until it is frozen. Stir well or beat again with a hand whisk.

6 Serve the ice cream sprinkled with chopped toasted almonds and decorated with small sprigs of fresh lavender.

Serves 6

Variations

You can omit the lavender and add different flavourings to the basic vanilla ice cream.

1 Purée and sieve uncooked summer fruits, such as strawberries, raspberries or peaches, and stir into the cooked custard with the whipped cream.

2 After folding the whipped cream into the vanilla custard, fold in 115 g/4 oz of grated chocolate — use only the best-quality

bitter chocolate, which has a high cocoa solids content.

3 Use cinnamon sticks instead of lavender to infuse the cream, and add a teaspoon of ground cinnamon to the custard before freezing.

4 Cook and then purée and sieve some gooseberries. Stir into the custard with some elderflower cordial.

Orange Granita

An Italian granita differs from a sorbet in that it is more grainy in texture and comprised of frozen crystals. It is a very refreshing summer dessert. For this recipe, it is best to use the juice of freshly squeezed oranges rather than juice from a carton.

450 ml/³/₄ pint fresh orange juice

3-4 tablespoons granulated sugar

sprigs of fresh mint, to decorate

1 Pour the orange juice and sugar into a blender or food processor and process briefly. Pour into a freezer container and then freeze the granita until half frozen.

2 Remove from the freezer and stir well to break up the ice crystals. Return to the freezer for 30 minutes, then remove and stir again.

3 Repeat this stirring process every 30 minutes over the next 3-4 hours, then remove from the freezer and serve in tall glasses or goblets.

Serves 6-8

Caribbean **Sorbet**

If wished, you can add a little white rum to the sorbet mixture before freezing. If guavas are not available, use mangoes or papayas instead.

2-3 ripe guavas, peeled and sliced
150 g/5 oz sugar
400 ml/14 fl oz water
5 ripe bananas, peeled and sliced
juice of 2 limes
chocolate sauce, to serve (see below)

1 Put the guavas, sugar and water in a saucepan and simmer gently over low heat, until the fruit is tender. Add the bananas and simmer for about 5 minutes, until softened.

2 Allow to cool a little, then sieve to remove the pips. When completely cold, stir in the lime juice.

3 Pour the sieved fruit mixture into a freezer container and freeze until half-frozen. Remove from the freezer and stir well or beat with a hand whisk. Replace in the freezer until the sorbet is frozen.

4 Serve the sorbet in scoops in a pool of cold chocolate sauce.

Serves 6

Christmas Sorbet

Serve this fresh, citrusy sorbet at Christmas, especially after rich and heavy meals. It tastes particularly good with chocolate sauce.

300 g/10 oz sugar
600 ml/1 pint water
6 cloves
9 large satsumas, tangerines or clementines

FOR THE CHOCOLATE SAUCE:
225 g/8 oz bitter plain chocolate
115 ml/4 fl oz double cream
115 ml/4 fl oz milk
25 g/1 oz caster sugar

1 Put the sugar, water and cloves in a saucepan. Heat gently, stirring all the time until the sugar dissolves and the liquid is clear.

2 Bring to the boil, and boil for 2-3 minutes until the syrup thickens. Set aside until the syrup is cold, then remove the cloves.

3 Squeeze the juice from 8 satsumas and stir into the cold sugar syrup. Pour into a freezing container and freeze for 2-3 hours, until half-frozen. Then remove from the freezer and beat with a hand whisk. Replace in the freezer until the sorbet has frozen solid.

4 Meanwhile, make the chocolate sauce. Break the chocolate into pieces and place them in a bowl over a saucepan of simmering water, until the chocolate melts. Remove from the heat.

5 Put the double cream, milk and sugar in a saucepan and bring to the boil, stirring all the time. Stir into the melted chocolate and then set aside the chocolate sauce to cool.

6 Serve the frozen sorbet in scoops in a pool of cold chocolate sauce, decorated with peeled segments from the remaining satsuma.

Serves 6

Baking

In the kitchen, there is nothing more wonderful than the aroma of freshly baked bread and cakes. Home baking can play an important role in today's contemporary, healthy vegetarian diet, and there are lots of recipes for delicious and unusual breads, teabreads, scones and cakes in this chapter. Baking is very enjoyable and therapeutic as well as being surprisingly easy.

Basic White **Bread**

1.5 kg/3 lb strong white
bread flour
4 teaspoons salt
25 g/1 oz vegetable margarine
2 teaspoons sugar
2 x 14 g packets easy-blend yeast
200 ml/7 fl oz milk
500 ml/17 fl oz water
milk or beaten egg, for glazing

FOR THE ITALIAN
GARLIC BREAD:
25 g/1 oz sun-dried tomatoes
in oil, chopped
2 garlic cloves, crushed
50 g/2 oz black olives, stoned
and chopped
3 tablespoons tomato purée

FOR THE CHEESE AND
HERB BREAD:
50 g/2 oz grated Cheddar cheese
1 teaspoon dried thyme
1 small red chilli, seeded
and chopped

This basic bread recipe can be flavoured in many ways, and two delicious variations are given below. If wished, you can make rolls instead of loaves, in which case you should shorten the baking time to 18-20 minutes.

1 Sift the white bread flour and salt into a large mixing bowl. Cut the margarine into small pieces and rub into the flour. Stir in the sugar and easy-blend yeast. Heat the milk and water until hand-hot, then mix into the flour to form a soft dough.

2 Turn out on to a lightly floured surface and knead well for 5-10 minutes, until the dough is elastic and smooth. Put the dough in a lightly oiled bowl, cover and leave in a warm place for about 1 hour, until well risen and doubled in size.

3 Knock the dough down with your fists and divide into 3 pieces. Shape one piece of dough into a loaf and place in a well-greased loaf tin. Cover with a clean tea-towel and set aside in a warm place to 'prove'.

4 Roll out the second piece of dough. Mix all the Italian garlic filling ingredients together and spread over the dough. Roll up and pat into a loaf. Place in a greased loaf tin. Cover and leave in a warm place.

5 Roll out the remaining dough and sprinkle with the cheese and herb filling. Roll up and place in a greased loaf tin or shape into rolls. Cover and leave in a warm place.

6 When the dough rises to the top of the tins, brush lightly with a little milk or beaten egg and bake in a preheated oven at 220°C, 425°F, Gas Mark 7 for about 30 minutes. When the loaves are ready, they will sound hollow when you tap the bottoms. Cool on a wire rack.

Makes 3 loaves

Basic White Bread

Italian **Focaccia**

This flat bread can be made into small loaves or rolls, topped with fruity olive oil. You can also experiment with different toppings.

FOR THE DOUGH:
450 g/1 lb plain flour
1/2 teaspoon salt
1 teaspoon brown sugar
3 teaspoons easy-blend yeast
300 ml/1/2 pint warm water
2 tablespoons olive oil

1 Sift the flour and salt into a large mixing bowl. Stir in the brown sugar and yeast, and then make a well in the centre of the flour.

2 Pour in the warm water and olive oil and mix well to form a soft dough. Turn out on to a lightly floured surface and knead for 10 minutes, until the dough is silky and elastic.

3 Put the dough in an oiled bowl, cover with cling film or a tea towel, and leave in a warm place until well risen and doubled in size.

4 Turn out the dough and punch it down. Knead lightly, then either roll the dough out to a large oval or a rectangle, or cut into 4 pieces and roll out each one individually. Prick the dough all over with a fork and place on an oiled baking sheet.

5 Add the topping of your choice and bake in a preheated oven at 220°C, 425°F, Gas Mark 7: 20 minutes for a large loaf, 15 minutes for smaller ones. Do not allow the toppings to brown or burn. Reduce the oven temperature to 190°C, 375°F, Gas Mark 5 if necessary. The cooked focaccia should look crisp and golden. Cool on a wire rack.

Makes 1 large loaf or 4 small ones

Olive and garlic topping

75 g/3 oz mixed black and green olives
3-4 garlic cloves, peeled and thinly sliced
10-12 fresh basil leaves
1 teaspoon coarse sea salt crystals
2 tablespoons olive oil

Press the olives and slivers of garlic lightly into the dough. Tear each basil leaf into 2 or 3 pieces and push them into the dough. Sprinkle with sea salt and drizzle with olive oil.

Sun-dried tomato topping

2 tablespoons sun-dried tomatoes in oil, chopped
1 tablespoon roughly chopped fresh sage
freshly ground mixed peppercorns (green, black, red)
2 tablespoons olive oil

Scatter the sun-dried tomatoes over the dough and press them in lightly. Sprinkle with sage and the freshly ground peppercorns, then drizzle the olive oil over the top.

Rosemary topping

2 tablespoons fresh rosemary leaves
1 teaspoon coarse sea salt crystals
2 tablespoons olive oil

Scatter the rosemary and sea salt over the dough, then drizzle the olive oil over the top.

Provençal **Olive** Bread

For a really authentic flavour, try to obtain some small black or purple Niçois olives. Otherwise, use oil-cured Italian, Greek or Spanish olives.

675 g/1½ lb strong white bread flour
2 teaspoons salt
1 x 14 g packet easy-blend yeast
400 ml/14 fl oz warm water
4 tablespoons olive oil
175 g/6 oz black olives, pitted and roughly chopped

1 Sift the flour and salt into a large mixing bowl, mix in the easy-blend yeast and make a well in the centre.

2 Pour in the warm water and olive oil and mix well with your hand, drawing in the flour from the sides of the bowl. You should end up with a soft ball of dough that leaves the bowl clean.

3 Knead the dough for about 10 minutes on a lightly floured surface, until it is silky and elastic. Place in an oiled bowl, cover with some cling film or a clean tea-towel and leave in a warm place until well risen and doubled in size.

4 Punch down the dough to remove the air bubbles. Press it out with your hands and sprinkle with the black olives. Fold the dough over the olives and knead well to distribute them evenly throughout.

5 Cut the dough in half and shape each piece into a round loaf. Place the loaves on an oiled baking sheet, cover with a clean tea-towel and leave in a warm place for about 30 minutes, until doubled in size.

6 Bake the loaves in a preheated oven at 220°C, 425°F, Gas Mark 7 for 25-30 minutes. If the loaves are browning too quickly, lower the oven temperature to 200°C, 400°F, Gas Mark 6 after 15 minutes. Cool the loaves on a wire rack.

Makes 2 loaves

Thyme, Onion and Garlic **Bread**

This fragrant bread, flavoured with garlic and herbs, is the perfect partner to cheese, olives and little Mediterranean gherkins.

350 g/12 oz wholemeal flour
½ teaspoon salt
2 teaspoons fresh thyme leaves
1 small onion, finely chopped
2 garlic cloves, crushed
½ x 7 g packet easy-blend yeast
200 ml/7 fl oz warm milk and water
2 tablespoons olive oil
1 egg, beaten

1 Sift the flour and salt into a mixing bowl and stir in the thyme, onion, garlic and easy-blend yeast. Make a well in the centre and pour in the warm milk and water, olive oil and beaten egg. Mix to form a ball of soft dough which leaves the sides of the bowl clean.

2 Turn the dough out on to a lightly floured board and knead for about 10 minutes, until the dough is really elastic. Place in an oiled bowl, cover and leave in a warm place until well risen and doubled in size.

3 Knock the dough back to get rid of any air bubbles. Knead lightly and shape into a loaf. Place in a well-greased 450-g/1-lb loaf tin, cover with a clean cloth and leave to rise in a warm place.

4 Bake the loaf in a preheated oven at 230°C, 450°F, Gas Mark 8 for about 30 minutes. Remove from the tin and cool on a wire rack.

Makes 1 loaf

Variations

1 Make the dough, omitting the thyme, onion and garlic. After rising and knocking back, mix 1 tablespoon crushed red and green peppercorns into the dough.

2 Add 115 g/4 oz mixed sunflower, pumpkin and poppy seeds to the flour and yeast mixture before adding the warm liquid.

Granary loaves

Serves 6

These moist, nutty loaves stay fresh for several days, and can be frozen successfully. You can bake a large batch and freeze any loaves you do not want to eat immediately. If wished, you can use two 7-g packets of easy-blend yeast rather than fresh yeast. Of course, you can simplify the process and make the bread in a food processor or food mixer if you have a special dough attachment or a dough hook.

1.5 kg/3 lb malted granary flour
4 teaspoons salt
50 g/2 oz vegetable margarine, diced
115 g/4 oz cracked wheat
25 g/1 oz wheatgerm
50 g/2 oz bran
2 tablespoons brown sugar
2 tablespoons molasses
900 ml/1½ pints warm water
40 g/1½ oz fresh yeast
beaten egg or milk, to glaze
cracked wheat, for decoration

1 Sift the flour and salt into a large mixing bowl, and then rub in the margarine until thoroughly blended. Next, stir in the cracked wheat, wheatgerm, bran and brown sugar.

2 Stir the molasses into the warm water and add 2 tablespoons of the mixture to the fresh yeast. Stir well to mix. Make a well in the centre of the flour mixture and pour in the yeast and warm water. Mix well to form a smooth dough that leaves the sides of the bowl clean.

3 Turn the dough out on to a lightly floured surface and knead for 10

minutes, until it is really smooth, silky and elastic. When kneading, always fold the dough inwards towards you with one hand while pushing it away from you with the other. Give the dough a quarter-turn and repeat. Place the dough in an oiled bowl, cover with some cling film or a clean tea-towel, and leave in a warm place until well risen and doubled in size.

4 Punch the dough down with your fists to knock out any air bubbles, and knead lightly. Cut into 3 pieces and shape into loaves. Place them on a well-greased baking tray, cover with a clean tea-towel and leave in a warm place until doubled in size. Alternatively, you can shape the dough into loaves and place each one in a well-greased 450-g/1-lb loaf tin, and leave in a warm place until the dough rises to the top of the tins. Or you can make plaited loaves or rolls. Glaze the loaves with beaten egg or milk, and sprinkle with cracked wheat. Bake in a preheated oven at 230°C, 450°F, Gas Mark 8 for 30-35 minutes. If the bases sound hollow when tapped with your knuckles, then the loaves are cooked. Cool on a wire rack.

Baileys Cheese **Scones**

These delicious cheese scones are the speciality of Baileys Tearooms in Bury St Edmunds and are best served warm, split and buttered.

450 g/1 lb self-raising flour
2 level teaspoons baking powder
115 g/4 oz soft margarine or butter
225 g/8 oz Cheddar cheese, grated
2 heaped teaspoons
whole-grain mustard
115 ml/4 fl oz milk, to mix
2 teaspoons sesame seeds

1 Sift the flour and baking powder into a mixing bowl, and rub in the margarine or butter. Stir in the grated cheese and mustard.

2 Add sufficient milk to form a workable soft dough, and then turn out on to a lightly floured surface.

3 Lightly roll out the dough, about 4 cm/1½ in thick. Cut into rounds with a 5-cm/2-in cutter, and place on a baking sheet. Leave to rest for 10 minutes, then brush the tops with milk and sprinkle with sesame seeds.

4 Bake near the top of a preheated oven at 200°C, 400°F, Gas Mark 6 for 12-15 minutes, until risen and golden brown. Cool slightly on a wire rack before serving.

Makes 20 scones

Carrot and Herb **Muffins**

225 g/8oz wholemeal
self-raising flour
pinch of salt
1 teaspoon baking powder
50 g/2 oz butter, softened
115 g/4 oz grated Swiss or
Cheddar cheese
1 carrot, grated
1 onion, grated
small bunch snipped chives
1 egg, beaten
115 ml/ 4 fl oz milk

These savoury little muffins are flavoured with cheese, carrot, onion and fresh herbs. They are ideal for brunches, picnics and high teas. If wished, you can split and butter them.

1 Sift the flour, salt and baking powder into a mixing bowl, and rub in the butter with your fingertips. Mix in 75 g/3 oz of the grated cheese, with the carrot and onion, then stir in the chives.

2 Stir in the beaten egg and milk to bind the mixture. Divide between 8 paper cases or 8 buttered deep muffin tins. Sprinkle lightly with the remaining grated cheese.

3 Bake in a preheated oven at 200°C, 400°F, Gas Mark 6 for about 15 minutes, until the muffins are risen and golden. Cool on a wire rack before serving.

Makes 8 muffins

Old-fashioned **Shortbread**

This delicious shortbread is made with healthy wholemeal flour.

115 g/4 oz butter, diced
150 g/5 oz wholemeal flour
25 g/1 oz rice flour or semolina
50 g/2 oz soft brown sugar
caster sugar, for dredging

1 Rub the butter into the wholemeal and rice flours, and stir in the brown sugar. Mix to a firm dough, then knead on a lightly floured board.

2 Roll out the dough to a large round, 5 mm/¼ in thick, and place on a baking sheet. Prick all over with a fork.

3 Bake in a preheated oven at 180°C, 350°F, Gas Mark 4 for 20-25 minutes. Cut into triangles while the shortbread is warm and leave to cool. Dredge with caster sugar.

Makes 12 triangles

Apricot Slices

Afternoon tea is one of life's great pleasures. These apricot slices are just the thing at dusk on a cold winter's afternoon in front of a blazing fire.

115 g/4 oz dried apricots
115 g/4 oz wholemeal flour
pinch of salt
115 g/4 oz rolled oats
25 g/1 oz wheatgerm
150 g/5 oz butter, softened
75 g/3 oz dark Barbados sugar
50 g/2 oz soft brown
Muscovado sugar
50 g/2 oz desiccated coconut
1 teaspoon bicarbonate of soda
2 teaspoons boiling water

1 Put the apricots in a bowl, cover with water and leave to soak for about 2 hours. Transfer to a small saucepan and simmer gently over low heat for about 10 minutes, or until softened but still firm. Drain the apricots and set aside.

2 Put the flour, salt, rolled oats and wheatgerm in a mixing bowl. Rub in the butter, then stir in the sugars and coconut. Dissolve the bicarbonate of soda in the boiling water and stir into the crumble mixture.

3 Press half of the crumble mixture into a buttered 20-cm/8-in square shallow baking tin. Press down well to cover the base and level it. Then spread the drained, cooked apricots evenly over the top. Cover with the remaining crumble mixture and press down firmly, smoothing out the surface.

4 Bake in a preheated oven at 180°C, 350°F, Gas Mark 4 for 30-35 minutes, until cooked and the top is golden brown. Cool in the tin and then cut into 12 slices.

Makes 12 slices

Banana Bread

This is served for breakfast throughout the Caribbean archipelago of islands. However, you can serve it sliced and buttered for afternoon tea.

115 g/4 oz butter, softened
175 g/6 oz caster sugar
2 eggs
3 large ripe bananas, peeled
and mashed
75 g/3 oz coarsely chopped pecans
225 g/8 oz self-raising flour
1/2 teaspoon salt
1/2 teaspoon nutmeg
good pinch of cinnamon
few drops of vanilla essence
1/2 teaspoon bicarbonate of soda

1 Cream the butter and sugar in a mixing bowl. Beat in the eggs, one at a time. Stir in the mashed bananas and pecans, then sift the flour, salt and spices into the mixture. Fold in gently, then stir in the vanilla essence and bicarbonate of soda.

2 Line a buttered 450-g/1-lb loaf tin with greaseproof paper, and spoon the banana mixture into the tin. Level the top, and then bake in a preheated oven at 180°C, 350°F, Gas Mark 4 for about 1 hour. Test whether the banana bread is cooked by inserting a metal skewer into the centre. It is ready when the skewer comes out clean.

3 Allow the banana bread to cool in the tin for 10 minutes, and then turn out the loaf on to a wire rack. When it is completely cold, cut into slices to serve. The banana bread keeps well, wrapped in kitchen foil, for several days. It also freezes successfully.

Makes 1 loaf

Date and **Walnut** Loaf

This is a really old-fashioned loaf to serve at afternoon tea. Wrap it up in foil and it will stay moist and delicious for several days.

225 ml/8 fl oz water
175 g/6 oz soft brown
Muscovado sugar
25 g/1 oz butter
1 teaspoon bicarbonate of soda
115 g/4 oz dates, chopped
2 eggs, beaten
225 g/8 oz plain or wholemeal flour
115 g/4 oz chopped walnuts

1 Bring the water to the boil in a saucepan, then add the sugar, butter, bicarbonate of soda and dates. Reduce the heat and stir gently over low heat until the sugar dissolves.

2 Remove the pan from the heat, allow to cool a little and then stir in the beaten eggs. Mix thoroughly and then add the flour and chopped walnuts.

3 Butter a 450-g/1-lb loaf tin and then line it with greaseproof paper. Pour the date and walnut mixture into the lined tin and bake in a preheated oven at 190°C, 375°F, Gas Mark 5 for 25-30 minutes, until risen and golden brown.

4 Leave the loaf in the tin for about 10 minutes, and then turn out on to a wire rack to cool. When cold, serve sliced and buttered.

Makes 1 loaf

Zucchini Nut Loaf

3 eggs
175 g/6 oz soft Molasses
brown sugar
115 ml/4 fl oz sunflower
or walnut oil
150 g/5 oz wholemeal flour
150 g/5 oz plain flour
1 heaped teaspoon baking powder
1/2 teaspoon bicarbonate of soda
1 teaspoon cinnamon
1/2 teaspoon allspice
1/2 teaspoon ground ginger
pinch of salt
2 medium courgettes, finely grated
50 g/2 oz chopped dates
50 g/2 oz chopped hazelnuts or
walnuts

Here's an unusual spicy tea-loaf with a difference. Made with oil instead of butter and flecked with grated green courgettes, it is delicious served sliced and buttered for afternoon tea.

1 Beat the eggs, sugar and oil in a mixing bowl or food processor until well blended. Gently fold in the sifted flours, baking powder, bicarbonate of soda, spices and salt. Fold in the grated courgettes, having squeezed out any moisture, dates and chopped hazelnuts.

2 Butter a 450-g/1-lb loaf tin and line with greaseproof paper. Pour in the mixture and level the top. Bake in a preheated oven at 180°C, 350°F, Gas Mark 4 for 1 1/4 hours, or until

well risen and golden. To test whether the loaf is cooked, insert a skewer in the centre – it should come out clean.

3 Cool in the tin for 10-15 minutes, then turn out on to a wire rack. Serve sliced and buttered.

Makes 1 loaf

Opposite: Date and Walnut Loaf (in the foreground) and Zucchini Nut Loaf

Sticky **Ginger** Cake

115 g/4 oz butter, softened
115 g/4 oz dark brown
molasses sugar
2 large eggs
225 g/8 oz plain flour
1 teaspoon baking powder
2 teaspoons ground ginger
1 teaspoon allspice
300 g/10 oz black treacle
115 g/4 oz stem ginger,
roughly chopped
1 teaspoon bicarbonate of soda
3 tablespoons warm milk

FOR THE ICING:
juice of ¹/₂ lemon
115 g/4 oz icing sugar, sifted
stem ginger pieces, for decoration

Impossibly dark, wickedly sticky and unbelievably moist, this has to be the best ginger cake ever. It will keep for at least a week stored in an airtight container; indeed, it improves after a couple of days if you can bear to forgo eating it immediately.

1 Cream the butter and sugar in a bowl or a food processor. Beat in the eggs, one at a time, and then sift in the flour, baking powder and spices. Fold gently into the mixture.

2 Stir in the black treacle and stem ginger. Blend the bicarbonate of soda with the warm milk, and stir gently into the cake mixture. If the mixture is a bit too thick, you can thin it down with some more milk or a little more syrup from the stem ginger jar.

3 Butter and line a 17.5-cm/7-in round cake tin, and pour in the cake mixture. Bake in a preheated oven at 170°C, 325°F, Gas Mark 3 for 1¹/₄ hours, then lower the temperature to 150°C, 300°F, Gas Mark 2 for a further 30 minutes.

4 Allow the cake to cool in the tin and then turn it out. Don't worry if it sinks a little in the middle – just turn the cake over and prepare to ice the base instead of the top.

5 Mix the lemon juice and icing sugar to a smooth paste and spoon over the top of the cake so that the icing drizzles down the sides. Decorate with pieces of stem ginger.

Makes 1 cake

American Cranberry **Muffins**

75 g/3 oz dried cranberries
225 ml/8 fl oz milk or buttermilk
225 g/8 oz plain flour
1¹/₂ teaspoons baking powder
¹/₂ teaspoon salt
50 g/2 oz caster sugar
1 large egg, beaten
grated zest of 1 orange
50 g/2 oz butter, melted

FOR THE TOPPING:
50 g/2 oz chopped walnuts
40 g/1¹/₂ oz crushed amber
sugar crystals

These muffins are quick and easy to make. Serve them warm and fresh from the oven for breakfast or brunch in the American style. If wished, you can substitute dried blueberries for the cranberries.

1 Put the dried cranberries in a bowl and add the milk or buttermilk. Set aside to soak for 10-15 minutes.

2 Sift the flour and baking powder into a mixing bowl. Add the salt and sugar and stir well. Make a well in the centre of the flour.

3 Mix the beaten egg, orange zest and melted butter into the milk and cranberries. Pour into the well in the flour, and mix gently together.

4 Divide the muffin mixture between 12 paper cases or 12 well-buttered muffin tins. Sprinkle with the chopped walnuts and sugar crystals.

5 Bake in a preheated oven at 200°C, 400°F, Gas Mark 6 for 20 minutes, until well risen and golden. Cool for 10-15 minutes, then serve warm.

Makes 12 muffins

Opposite: American Cranberry Muffins

Basic Recipes

In the following pages you will find some useful basic recipes for sauces, dressings, salsas, pastry and croûtons. Many of these are referred to throughout this book, especially the classic vegetable stock, which forms the basis of many soups, stews and casseroles. The flavour is so superior to commercial stock cubes that it is well worth making in bulk and freezing until required.

Creamy **Mushroom** Sauce

350 g/12 oz mushrooms (chestnut,
girolles, chanterelles, ceps etc.)
75 g/3 oz butter
75 ml/3 fl oz Marsala
75 ml/3 fl oz vegetable stock
75-115 ml/3-4 fl oz cream
freshly ground black pepper

Serve this sauce with Layered Nut Roast (see page 74) or with any cooked pasta.

1 Slice the mushrooms thinly. Fry them in the butter in a large frying pan until golden brown.

2 Add the Marsala and vegetable stock and bring to the boil. Let the sauce bubble away until it reduces and starts to turn syrupy.

3 Stir in the cream and simmer gently for a few minutes. Season with freshly ground black pepper.

Makes 175 ml/6 fl oz

Garlic Croûtons

Serve these with vegetable soups or sprinkled over crisp green salads.

1 Cut the crusts off the bread and cut it into small cubes. Put them in a bowl with the olive oil and garlic and toss gently together.

2 Arrange the croûtons on a baking tray and place in a preheated oven at

4 thick slices crusty white bread
2 tablespoons fruity green
olive oil
2 garlic cloves, crushed

180°C, 350°F, Gas Mark 4 for 8-10 minutes, until crisp and golden. Check them from time to time to

Variation

For herb croûtons, substitute 1-2 tablespoons finely chopped fresh herbs for the garlic cloves, and proceed as described.

make sure that they do not become too brown. Remove and cool.

Fresh **Avocado** Sauce

1 large ripe avocado
2 tablespoons mayonnaise
175 ml/6 fl oz low-fat fromage frais
dash of lemon juice

Serve this quick and easy sauce with vegetable burgers, or pile into split pitta breads with salad.

Peel and stone the avocado, and then mash the flesh. Mix in the mayonnaise and fromage frais, and add lemon juice to taste. This sauce should be made soon before eating, or the avocado will discolour.

Makes 225 ml/8 fl oz

Creamy **Mayonnaise**

To make a perfect mayonnaise all the ingredients should be at room temperature. Add the oil very slowly – drop by drop and then in a thin stream – or the mayonnaise may curdle. If the worst happens and it does curdle, don't panic. Just break another egg yolk into a clean bowl and then slowly beat in the curdled mayonnaise.

2 egg yolks
good pinch of salt
1 tablespoon white wine vinegar
1 teaspoon powdered mustard
freshly ground black pepper
300 ml/^{1}/$_2$ pint olive oil
squeeze of lemon juice

1 Whisk the egg yolks, salt, wine vinegar, mustard and black pepper together in a large bowl, until well blended. Use a wire whisk or electric hand-held one

2 Start adding the olive oil, drop by drop, whisking all the time. When the sauce starts to thicken, add the remaining oil in a thin stream, still whisking all the time.

3 Stir in a tablespoon of boiling water and a squeeze of lemon juice. Store the mayonnaise in a covered container in the refrigerator.

Makes 300 ml/^{1}/$_2$ pint

Variations
....

You can flavour the basic mayonnaise with chopped fresh herbs (chives, dill, tarragon), crushed garlic cloves or chopped capers.

Vegetable **Stock**

900 ml/1 ^{1}/$_2$ pints water
2 onions, peeled and sliced
2 carrots, peeled and halved
1 leek, cleaned, trimmed and halved
2 celery sticks, halved
1 bay leaf
few parsley stalks
few sprigs of thyme
few celery leaves
10 black peppercorns
good pinch of salt

Use this stock for making stews, soups and casseroles, and in any recipes that call for stock. It has a stronger, better flavour than broths made with stock cubes. If wished, you can double the quantities given here, and freeze some stock for the future.

1 Put the water, vegetables, herbs and seasonings in a large saucepan.

2 Bring to the boil, then cover the pan and simmer very gently for 1^1/$_2$ hours. Strain and use.

Makes 600 ml/1 pint

Barbecue Sauce

Serve this tangy sauce with grilled vegetables and kebabs.

1 onion, finely chopped
2 garlic cloves, crushed
2 tablespoons olive oil
1 x 400-g/14-oz can chopped tomatoes
1 tablespoon white wine vinegar
1 tablespoon soft brown sugar

1/2 teaspoon cayenne pepper
1 teaspoon Dijon mustard
1 thick slice of lemon
2 tablespoons Worcestershire sauce
3 tablespoons tomato ketchup
1 tablespoon tomato purée
salt and freshly ground black pepper

1 Fry the onion and garlic gently in the oil until soft and golden. Add the canned tomatoes, vinegar, sugar, cayenne, mustard and lemon. Bring to the boil, then reduce the heat a little and cook vigorously for about 15 minutes, until the sauce thickens.

2 Add the remaining ingredients and continue cooking for another 5 minutes, or until thick. Remove the slice of lemon just before serving.

Makes 300 ml/1/2 pint

Exotic Fruit Salsa

1 ripe mango, peeled, stoned and diced
1 papaya, peeled, seeded and diced
450 g/1 lb ripe tomatoes, skinned, seeded and chopped
1 small red onion, finely chopped
1 red pepper, seeded and diced
2 hot red chillies, seeded and finely chopped
1 tablespoon olive oil
juice of 1 lime
salt and freshly ground black pepper
3 tablespoons chopped coriander leaves

You can serve this salsa with spicy Mexican and Indian dishes, grilled and barbecued vegetables, or simply with bread and cheese.

Mix the mango, papaya, tomatoes, onion, red pepper and chillies in a bowl. Add the olive oil and lime juice and toss together. Season to taste with salt and pepper, and stir in the coriander leaves.

Serves 4

Blue cheese pasta sauce

You can use any blue cheese (Stilton, Gorgonzola, Roquefort, etc.) in this rich, creamy sauce for pasta. For a quick meal, simply toss some tagliatelle, pappardelle or fettuccine in the sauce and serve with a crisp green salad.

450 ml/ 3/4 pint double cream
50 g/2 oz butter
115 g/4 oz blue cheese, cubed
salt and freshly ground black pepper

Pour the cream into a saucepan and heat through gently until it starts bubbling. Add the butter, reduce the heat and simmer gently for 10 minutes, until reduced and creamy. Stir in the blue cheese, season with salt and pepper, and toss with the pasta of your choice.

Serves 4

Classic **vinaigrette** dressing

This dressing will add interest to any green, mixed, tomato or potato salad. You can vary it in many ways as outlined below. The only hard and fast rule is that you must use good-quality olive oil.

3 tablespoons extra-virgin olive oil
1 tablespoon white wine vinegar
1 teaspoon Dijon mustard
pinch of caster sugar

Measure the olive oil and wine vinegar into a small bowl and blend together. Stir in the mustard and sugar, until thoroughly amalgamated.

Makes 50 ml/2 fl oz dressing

Variations

1 Substitute red wine vinegar, tarragon vinegar, cider vinegar, balsamic vinegar, lemon or lime juice for the white wine vinegar.

2 Add a crushed garlic clove and/or some finely chopped fresh herbs, especially chives and tarragon.

Guacamole

2 ripe avocados
juice of 1 small lime
2 garlic cloves, crushed
4 spring onions, finely chopped
1 hot green chilli, seeded and chopped
2 ripe tomatoes, skinned and finely chopped
2 tablespoons chopped fresh coriander
salt and freshly ground black pepper

Serve this spicy green sauce with Mexican dishes, as a dip with raw vegetables or tortilla chips, or mixed with olive oil and wine vinegar as a salad dresing. Add more chillies if you like really hot food.

Cut the avocados in half, and remove the peel and stones. Scoop out the flesh. Put the avocado in a bowl with the lime juice, and mash coarsely. Stir in the garlic, spring onions, chilli, tomatoes and coriander to make a thick sauce. Season to taste with salt and plenty of freshly ground black pepper.

Cover the bowl and refrigerate until required. The lime juice will help prevent the avocado discolouring, but the guacamole should be eaten within a few hours of making if you want it to look really fresh and a delicate creamy green.

Serves 4-6

Shortcrust pastry

Use this pastry for making sweet and savoury tarts and pies. If wished, you can flavour it with some grated cheese, chopped herbs, mustard, grated orange and lemon rind, or ground nuts.

225 g/8 oz plain flour
pinch of salt
115 g/4 oz margarine, at room temperature
3-4 tablespoons cold water, to mix

Sift the flour and salt into a large bowl. Cut the margarine into small pieces and rub into the flour with your fingertips until the mixture resembles fine breadcrumbs. Mix in the cold water with a round-bladed knife, until the mixture binds to form a soft, smooth dough that leaves the sides of the bowl clean. Wrap the dough in some foil or a polythene bag and leave to rest in the refrigerator for 30 minutes before rolling out.

Makes 225 g/8 oz pastry

Index

The Vegetarian Society

The Vegetarian Society exists to promote, and provide information on, a vegetarian diet for the benefit of animal welfare, human health and the environment. Established in 1847, the Society is the acknowledged expert on vegetarianism and all aspects relating to the diet, and produces information sheets, leaflets, videos and other material.

Members of the Society receive a full-colour, high quality magazine each quarter, a discount card offering discounts at establishments ranging from health food stores to restaurants and guesthouses, as well as a range of diverse services from fancy dress hire to roadside rescue, our unique seedling logo badge, reduced rate subscription to *BBC Vegetarian Good Food* or *Wildlife* magazines, and exclusive access to the Society's free information hotline. It offers all members the opportunity to get actively involved if desired, either through the Society's network of 150 local groups or through the Council of Trustees, elected from the members.

The Society runs its own cookery school, Cordon Vert, which provides day, weekend and week courses ranging from our Diploma course and professional tuition to leisure courses for the beginner and the adventurous cook who want to expand their repertoire.

The Society also works with major food manufacturers and retailers to improve the quality, quantity and variety of vegetarian food available, and administers its own licence scheme for approved products.

To receive further information write to:

The Vegetarian Society
Parkdale
Dunham Road
Altrincham
Cheshire, WA14 4QG
Or telephone and join by Credit Card on
0161 928 0793.
The E-Mail address is
info@vegsoc.demon.co.uk.